D

New PUNCHNEEDLE *embroidery*
· BASICS & FINISHING TECHNIQUES ·

CHARLOTTE DUDNEY

Creative Publishing
international

Acknowledgments

Like many women, I belong to a stitch group. We are accomplished artists, and we've been together for over ten years. Carolyn, Dot, Peggy, Janice, Marty, and Susan are precious friends who are much more than a stitch group to me. They provide encouragement, inspiration, and confidence. We love anything creative—quilting, cross-stitch, rug hooking, basket weaving, and appliqué—and we often take road trips to enrich our knowledge of an art form. In fact, I discovered punchneedle with my stitch group.

My work has been received with enthusiasm by many independent shops. Locally owned needlework shops and quilt shops offer many premium projects, supplies, and good instruction. I've enjoyed traveling to many of them all over the United States teaching and promoting punchneedle. Thank you for your hospitality.

Special thanks to Kathy Morrissey at the Stitch Niche in Arlington, Texas. In 2003 she introduced some of my punchneedle designs. Punchneedle is now arguably the fastest growing segment of the needlework industry.

Special thanks to Norden Crafts, who invited me to demonstrate punchneedle embroidery at my first national market in 2003. This was the beginning of my business and relationship with dedicated shop owners!

Special thanks to my family and especially my husband, Fred. They have worked behind the scenes lending support in so many ways. I'm grateful to my daughter, Laura, who teaches me every day that nothing is impossible.

Creative Publishing
international

Copyright 2007
Creative Publishing international
18705 Lake Drive East
Chanhassen, Minnesota 55317
1-800-328-3895
www.creativepub.com
All rights reserved

President/CEO: Ken Fund
Vice President/Sales & Marketing: Peter Ackroyd
Publisher: Winnie Prentiss
Executive Managing Editor: Barbara Harold
Acquisition Editors: Linda Neubauer,
    Deborah Cannarella
Production Managers: Laura Hokkanen, Linda Halls

Creative Director: Michele Lanci-Altomare
Senior Design Manager: Brad Springer
Design Managers: Jon Simpson, Mary Rohl
Director of Photography: Tim Himsel
Lead Photographer: Steve Galvin
Photo Coordinator: Joanne Wawra
Book Design: Laurie Young
Cover Design: Mary Rohl
Page Layout: Laurie Young
Illustrator: Deb Pierce
Photographers: Andrea Rugg, Peter Caley

Library of Congress Cataloging-in-Publication Data

Dudney, Charlotte
  New punchneedle embroidery : basics & finishing
techniques / Charlotte Dudney.
      p. cm.
Includes index.
  ISBN-13: 978-1-58923-299-0 (soft cover)
  ISBN-10: 1-58923-299-2 (soft cover)
  1. Embroidery--Patterns. 2. Punched work. I. Title.

TT771.D83 2007
746.44'041--dc22   2006100070

Printed in China
10 9 8 7 6 5 4 3 2 1

CONTENTS

Introduction   *4*

Punchneedle: Yesterday, Today, and Tomorrow   *5*

PUNCHNEEDLE BASICS   7

Supplies   *8*

The Needle   *11*

Preparing the Fabric   *15*

How to Punch   *17*

Color Effects and Pile Manipulation   *20*

Problems and Solutions   *23*

Fiber and Fabric Recommendations   *24*

PROJECTS   27

Duncan   *28*

This Little Piggy   *30*

Baa, Baa, Black Sheep   *32*

Peep, Peep   *34*

Westie on Alert   *36*

Bunny   *38*

This Is Not a Partridge   *40*

Blooming Heart   *42*

Spring Through My Window   *44*

Summer Through My Window   *46*

Fall Through My Window   *48*

Winter Through My Window   *50*

Bless Our Home   *52*

Guardian Angel   *54*

Laura   *56*

Bouquet of Flowers   *58*

Crossed Tulips   *60*

Trio of Hearts   *62*

FINISHING & FRAMING   65

Eyeglass Bag   *66*

Fabric Frames   *68*

Mounting in a Preset Opening   *70*

Mounting on Foam Core Board   *72*

Finish with Cording   *74*

Whipstitched Edge   *76*

Archival Framing   *78*

Appliqué Finishing   *80*

Resources   *82*

About the Author   *83*

PATTERNS   85

INTRODUCTION

I love many forms of handwork: quilting, cross-stitch, rug hooking, basket weaving, and woodworking. It amazes me to see what I can make with my hands! One month our stitch group invited Leslie McCabe, an accomplished needle artist from Massachusetts, to join us. We all loved her unique style of rug hooking and use of color. She also introduced us to punchneedle embroidery. It was there that I fell in love with this miniature form of rug hooking. It was fun and easy. I learned that punchneedle projects can have dimension and texture and are much less expensive than traditional rug hooking.

Punchneedle can fit a busy lifestyle. You can work on a punchneedle project almost anywhere—on vacation, waiting in the dentists' office, or even in the car (as a passenger, of course!). Just use your needle and floss as you would a paint brush.

Punchneedle has many wonderful applications. Of course, most designs are suitable for framing. But you can also incorporate them into clothing embellishments or projects such as Christmas stockings, pins, purses, and so much more.

Since 2003, I've been teaching and promoting punchneedle in dozens of states. I can't tell you how many times during my travels someone has come up to me and said, "I've had this punchneedle for years and never learned how to use it." I've taught children to punch. I've taught elderly women with arthritis. I've taught people with disabilities. I've even taught my husband! Just about anyone can learn to enjoy punchneedle with proper instruction. My goal is for you to be confident in the art form of punchneedle embroidery.

Read through the Punchneedle Basics section first to learn about all the tools, materials, and techniques for punchneedle. If you have some experience with punchneedle, refer to this section to refresh your memory and to learn a few new tricks. Also watch for my special tips throughout the book to make your projects easier.

In the Projects section, I have included 20 new designs for your punchneedle enjoyment. They vary in style, size, and subject—something for every occasion and purpose. All the patterns are provided full size beginning on page 85.

When you finish punching your design, what do you do with it? You will want to showcase your design in some special way and preserve it. The Finishing and Framing section, beginning on page 65, presents almost every finishing technique I know. Choose one or a combination of techniques to give your project the perfect finishing touch.

I have really enjoyed creating this book, and I hope it brings you many hours of enjoyment, too. Happy punching!

Charlotte Dudney

PUNCHNEEDLE: YESTERDAY, TODAY, AND TOMORROW

Punchneedle may seem like a new form of needle art. But it's actually been around for centuries. To understand its history, you need to know about the Old Believers of seventeenth-century Russia.

Also known as Eastern Orthodox, Old Ritualists, and Old Orthodox, these people are a remnant of the Russian Orthodox Church. Hundreds of years ago, the Russian Orthodox Church was in a period of change. This group was called Old Believers because they did not accept the new ways. They eventually became persecuted for their defiance and had to flee Russia. Out of necessity, they formed closed groups much like the Amish of today.

Many Old Believers migrated to China, and later to Brazil and Argentina. Some came to the United States through European countries. In the 1960s, a group of Old Believers were given asylum by (then) Attorney General Robert Kennedy and moved to Woodburn, Oregon. When outsiders began influencing their children, a group of Old Believers left that community and moved to remote areas of Alaska. At first glance, you might think they are Amish: The men are bearded with dark clothing. The women wear long skirts and distinctive hats. However, unlike the Amish, they use many of the conveniences of modern life, such as cars and cell phones.

A unique aspect of their culture is the embroidery that we call punchneedle. The brightly colored embroidery appears in their clothing and religion. Men will wear embroidery on their shirts (from a distance it looks like a flowered necktie) or collar. Draperies that adorn their religious icons are also embellished with this embroidery. All these embroidered projects are produced by hand using a tiny needle and a single strand of floss.

In the summer of 2006, my husband and I traveled to Woodburn to investigate their culture and, specifically, their needlework. We were thrilled to see numerous Old Believer churches and interview several Old Believer practitioners. The churches are different from your typical American house of worship. They all have a distinctive onion dome (sometimes several). The outer paintings are very colorful. From a closer view you can see the Slavonic writings and pictures of their saints on the exterior. Many of the nearby homes have pictures of the Last Supper displayed prominently in the windows.

We especially wanted to speak with some Old Believer women who could tell us about the embroidery. We spoke to

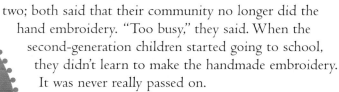

two; both said that their community no longer did the hand embroidery. "Too busy," they said. When the second-generation children started going to school, they didn't learn to make the handmade embroidery. It was never really passed on.

Although it still appears in their clothing and religion, most of the embroidery is now machine-made. I was able to find a beautiful handmade piece punched by Brazilian Old Believers. For this community, though, it seems that the handmade embroidery that they were once known for is a lost art.

The inventors of the craft have, for the most part, set punchneedle aside. That makes the resurgence of punchneedle embroidery in many parts of the world both significant and ironic. In quilt shops, needlework shops, and other specialty shops in the United States and Canada, people are learning punchneedle embroidery every day for its pure enjoyment. It has lots of appeal to today's busy needle-art enthusiasts, including portability and quickness. "New Believers" embrace punchneedle not for reasons of tradition or ritual, but for its own sake. We just love the simple joy of creating the colorful projects by hand.

In mainstream America and around the world, the art form has been growing in popularity. Five years ago, there very few artists producing ready-made patterns for punchneedle. Today, dozens of talented punchneedle designers make patterns. Punchneedle figures prominently in needlework magazines, quilt shops, needlework shops, and needle-art trade shows. It's even starting to show up in the mass market. Who knows, it may survive another 300 years.

PUNCHNEEDLE

Basics

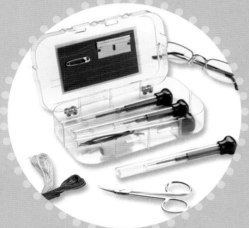

SUPPLIES

Punchneedle is a unique needle art. A special needle, threaded with floss, is punched down into the fabric from the wrong side. A small loop is left behind on the right side when the needle is brought up out of the fabric. In no time at all, a lush cluster of loops forms a "miniature rug." This amazing needle can even create different levels of pile for a three-dimensional look. The process is so easy, it won't be long before you feel confident enough to create your own designs. Punchneedle is also affordable. Here's all you need to get started:

- punchneedle with threader *(patterns in this book use the three-strand needle)*
- hoop with a locking lip
- weaver's cloth
- .05 acid-free Pigma pen
- small curved-tip scissors
- embroidery floss
- small storage case
- woven interfacing *(for fabrics other than weaver's)*
- good lighting

The Punchneedle and Threader

There are three main sizes of punchneedles—one-strand, three-strand, and six-strand—and there are many brands. Each has its own advantages and limitations. Here are some features to consider when buying a punchneedle.

Punchneedles come in many lengths and widths. Do you like a thin, medium, or fat handle? It's a matter of personal preference. My favorite needle is the CTR Punch Embroidery needle. The same size as a pencil, it is comfortable and easy to use.

Some needles use a set mechanical adjustment to change the depths of the stitch. Others use plastic gauge segments that you can remove or add to the needle. These can be adjusted to your personal preference. In my experience, punchers like to have options to their pile depths.

Some punchneedles have unique features. For example, Bernadine's Needle Art makes a needle with a small hexagonal handle—it won't roll off when placed on a table. CTR Needleworks needles feature a bevel indicator that easily shows the direction of the stitch.

Fine wire threaders are essential for loading the floss into the needle. They are normally included when you purchase a punchneedle.

The Hoop

For punchneedle embroidery, the fabric is stretched taut in a hoop, and the entire design must fit inside the hoop. Hoop-La by Susan Bates are the most affordable hoops for punchneedle. The inner ring has a lip edge that secures the fabric so that you can stretch it tight. The limitation is the size. I don't recommend using a hoop larger than 8" (20.3 cm) in diameter because it is difficult to keep the fabric tight. For punchneedle, the fabric must be drum tight.

Morgan hoops are sold individually and in a "lap frame" form. This hoop has a tongue-and-groove design that holds the fabric very tight. This is a great hoop for use with wool and thicker fabrics. You can also use larger sizes with this style of hoop.

A stretcher frame is a great alternative to a hoop. It's a smaller version of a traditional rug-hooking frame. Carding strips are on all four sides of the wooden frame. The fabric is stretched and laid over the carding. When you release the fabric over the carding, it grips the weave of the fabric. It is the best and easiest way to stretch your weaver's cloth. It doesn't leave a ring impression on your fabric and doesn't need to be adjusted. I love my "Round About Punchneedle Frame" made by K's Creations. You can order custom sizes or use the standard frame for all the designs in this book.

Weaver's Cloth

Weaver's cloth is the best fabric for punchneedle. Made of 45 percent cotton and 55 percent polyester, it comes in an assortment of colors. It is very durable and can be used with the one-strand, three-strand, and six-strand punchneedles. Natural or khaki weaver's cloth is available at most fabric stores. Weeks Dye Works overdyed weaver's cloth is available at needle-art shops.

Embroidery Floss

You can use a variety of fibers in your punchneedle. If the fiber flows freely through the shaft of the needle, it will produce the desired loops in your project. See page 24 for fiber

recommendations. I often use a variety of embroidery flosses to achieve the effect that I am looking for. Wool, silk, and cotton are all wonderful and can be found as solid and overdyed colors. When I discovered overdyed floss, I felt that I was painting with watercolored floss. The color palette is premixed and ready to be placed on your canvas. There are many beautiful colors and fibers to choose from.

Curve-Tip Scissors

It's important to have sharp, high-quality, 3½" (8.9 cm), curve-tip scissors for punchneedle. They are critical for the different thread manipulation techniques, such as clipping, sculpting, and shearing. I recommend the ones made by Gingher. The fine, curved tip allows you to get inside the loop to clip the threads.

Small Storage Case

You can organize and protect your punchneedle supplies with an accessories case. My favorite is the Haystack made by CTR Needleworks. The clear plastic case features a magnetic lid to help keep track of the threaders. It is large enough to hold needles, threaders, extra gauge segments, scissors, and more. The Haystack is designed to stay closed if dropped.

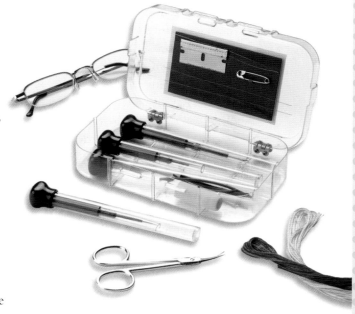

Woven Interfacing

If you want to punch on other fabrics, such as 100 percent cotton, wool, or knit fabric, you must stabilize them with woven interfacing. These fabrics stretch in all directions or do not have a distinguishable weave to punch on. Unlike weaver's cloth, they do not return to their original size when stretched. I use interfacing made by HTC called Form Flex All-Purpose. I've punched on canvas and denim bags, wool, and other fabrics. These are not beginner projects because the fabric is much harder to punch the needle into and requires good control of the needle. Make sure to cut a large enough piece so that the interfacing is well outside the hoop area. This will allow you to pull the stabilized fabric evenly. Follow the manufacturer's instructions when ironing on the interfacing.

Good Lighting

Good lighting is critical when working on your project. A true spectrum light is ideal. Direct the light so that you don't cast a shadow on the area you are stitching. If you are left-handed, you should have the light shining from your right. If you are right-handed, you should have the light shining from your left.

TIP
Be sure to let the interfacing cool to room temperature before placing it in the hoop. It will slip and come away from the fabric if it is still warm.

THE NEEDLE

It's all about the needle. This amazing tool has lots of unique features that control the depth and quality of your stitches. All you have to do is punch!

Choosing a Needle

You can use the needle over and over for years—in my experience, they get better with use—so don't hesitate to invest in a high-quality, all-metal needle. I use and instruct with the CTR series of punch embroidery needles. They are sold individually. If you only want to use the three-strand needle, you don't have to buy any other size. The three-strand is the most popular needle, and most designers use this size.

Beyond the handle, most punchneedles are very similar, with only a few exceptions. The essential parts of the needle are the diagonal slant at the tip of the needle called a "bevel" and an "eye" on the opposite side of the shaft.

The CTR needles have a bevel indicator, which is a huge benefit. You know where the bevel is at all times, even when it is depressed into the fabric. That is very important, as it determines the direction of a perfect stitch.

One of the wonderful features of the punchneedle is its ability to punch loops of various depths. Finished projects don't have to be flat. To achieve a multilevel effect, the punchneedle can

TIP
If your punchneedle does not have a bevel indicator, paint one on with red nail polish.

be adjusted to vary the pile depth. With some needles, gauge segments are attached to control the depth. Other needles have a built-in mechanical adjustment to control the depth.

Gauge segments are precut with the CTR punchneedle, but if you want to make even the slightest adjustment, it is very easy to change. Just place the plastic gauge on a self-healing mat. Using a sharp razor blade, make a straight vertical cut at the desired length.

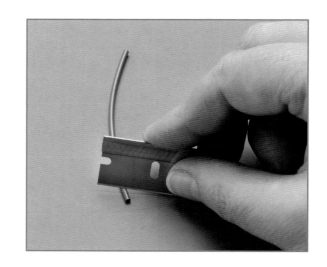

All About Gauge

When you punch the shaft of the needle into the fabric, it leaves behind a loop of floss on the opposite (front) side of the fabric. A punchneedle can leave long or short loops depending on the gauge setting. The gauge acts as a stopper that controls the penetration of the needle into the fabric and determines the size of loop that is left behind.

To determine the gauge measurement, place the middle of the needle eye on zero and measure the length of exposed shaft to the top of the gauge.

The chart below shows the different gauge measurements recommended for the three sizes of needles.

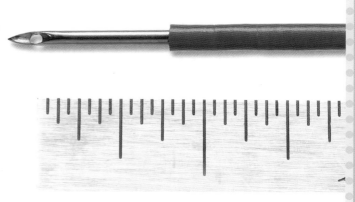

Recommended gauge setting*	One Strand	Three Strand	Six Strand
¼" (6 mm)	x		
⅜" (1 cm)	x	x	x
½" (1.3 cm)	x	x	x
⅝" (1.6 cm)		x	x
¾" (1.9 cm)			x

*Measured from the eye of the needle to the top of the gauge.

Different size needles can be used interchangeably in the same project as long as the gauges are adjusted to match. Line up the eyes of the needles to see if the gauges are even.

Needle Sizes

Needle sizes indicate how many strands of embroidery floss they can hold. A one-strand needle (1) is primarily used for detail because it uses a single strand of floss. It gives the overall design a much finer, elegant look, and even the smallest detail can be achieved with this amazing needle. Because it is the only size needle that was used by the Russian Old Believers, it is sometimes referred to as the Russian punchneedle.

The most popular size, the three-strand needle (2) is very versatile. You can use two or three strands of floss in this needle; therefore, you have the ability to mix colors. You can achieve a tweed background when you mix two strands of dark floss with one strand of light floss.

A six-strand needle (3) is used on projects that don't require a lot of detail. You can use four, five, or six strands of floss in this needle. With the larger shaft, it also allows you to use a number of different fibers that don't flow well through the one- or three-strand needles. However, there are a limited number of designs created for this needle.

Preparing the Floss

Pattern instructions tell you which size needle to use and how many strands of floss are needed. You will be using the three-strand needle for all the projects in this book. Cotton embroidery floss comes as six plys, or strands, loosely twisted together. You need to separate the six-ply floss into two segments of three strands each. There are two different ways to accomplish this:

METHOD 1. "Strip" one strand at a time from the floss by pinching the floss in one hand. Isolate one strand, and pull it gently from the bundle while continuing to pinch the main bundle. The main bundle will bunch up loosely as you pull, but will return to its original length when the single strand is completely free. After removing three single strands, gather them together again, twist them around your finger, and slide them through your hand. This will wind the strands into one unit and also allow you to make sure there are no snags in the floss.

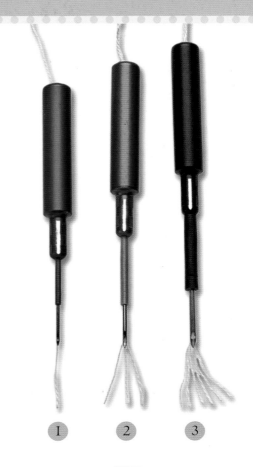

1   2   3

TIP
If you tend to fill design areas too tightly with loops or prefer a finer look, use only two strands in your three-strand needle. You will still achieve a beautiful lush pile.

METHOD 2. Pinch the top of the floss, and rake your finger over the tip of the floss, causing it to separate into two distinct sections. Gently separate the two sections, allowing the floss to dangle and unwind slowly. Have a partner hold the main line of floss as you pull the sections apart to keep the floss from tangling. Slide each section through your hand, letting it relax and checking for snags or knots.

Threading the Punchneedle

A long wire needle threader, usually supplied with the needle, is necessary for threading the needle. Typically, one end of the threader has a long narrow loop with a tiny twist at the end. The other end is soldered and rigid.

The needle is threaded in several steps. Not all threaders are the same, so be sure to check the manufacturer's instructions.

1. Insert the twisted loop end of the threader into the tip of the needle, and push it through the shaft until it comes out of the handle.
2. Insert the floss end through the narrow loop of the threader.
3. Pull the threader and floss through the shaft and out the tip of the needle. Continue pulling until the entire threader and a long length of floss are out.
4. Insert the soldered end of the threader through the eye of the needle from the beveled side, and pull it through the needle eye.
5. Pull the floss from the handle end until only a short tail of floss extends from the needle eye.

TIP

Place the threader back in its tube or on the magnetic holder inside the storage case right after you are finished. Threaders are very easy to lose.

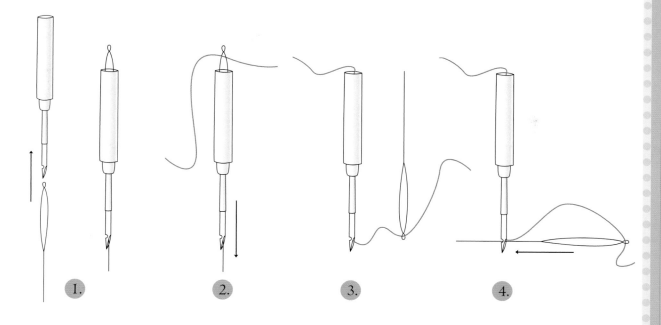

1.   2.   3.   4.

PREPARING THE FABRIC

Some punchneedle designs, like the ones in this book, are black line drawings that must be transferred to fabric. When transferring your design, orient it with the weft and warp—also called crosswise and lengthwise grain—of the weaver's cloth. The weft and warp of the fabric are very important to the size and proportion of your project. Fabric has slight "give" on the crosswise grain (weft) but is very stable on the lengthwise grain (warp). A design's proportion is determined by the way it is drawn on the fabric. You want your project to stretch the way it was intended, especially if it is designed to fit in a specific opening.

If you purchase traceable or iron-on patterns, be sure to follow the instructions for placing the design on the fabric. If a design does not indicate the orientation, you should align the longer side of the design with the warp, or lengthwise grain. If you place it the other way, the longer direction of your image will stretch and appear out of proportion.

Transferring the Design

The patterns in this book are printed as reverse images of the finished design. This is because the design is worked from the wrong side of the fabric. If you make your own designs, be sure to reverse the image when you draw the pattern. This is especially important if your design includes anything directional, such as text or numbers.

The back of each pattern page is blank, so you can easily transfer the design using a light box or sunny window. For accuracy, trace the design with a .05 acid-free Pigma pen.

1. Turn back the covers and pages of the book, and center the design pattern on the light box. Tape it in place along one edge.
2. Place the weaver's cloth over the pattern. Center the pattern under the fabric, and align the guides on the pattern to the warp and weft, as indicated.
3. Trace the lines using a .05 acid-free Pigma pen. Note how the borders of the design are perfectly aligned to the warp and weft of the fabric.

Placing the Fabric in a Hoop

Punching is much easier when the fabric is properly stretched in your hoop. The fabric must be drum tight, with the grain of the fabric running straight. When fabric is properly stretched in a Hoop-La hoop, it will become distorted and look more oval than round. This is normal.

1. Loosen the screw in the outer ring, and separate the two rings of the hoop.
2. Place the inner ring on the table. If using a Hoopla hoop, the lip edge should be on top. Place the fabric over the ring with the design facing up.
3. Slide the outer ring over the fabric and inner ring. If using a Hoop-La hoop, be sure to slide the outer ring over the lip edge of the inner ring until the lip rests on top. This lip edge secures the fabric as it is stretched. Tighten the screw with your fingers.
4. Pull the fabric side to side and top to bottom, keeping the grain of the fabric from becoming wavy. Each time you pull the fabric, tighten the screw. When you think you have stretched the fabric enough, stretch it a little more. When I teach classes and check my students' hoops, it amazes them when I can stretch their fabric a little more.

Placing the Fabric on a Stretcher Frame

If you have a stretcher frame, securing the fabric is much easier. You just stretch the fabric over the carding, and lay the fabric down. The carding grips the fabric when you let go. It's that easy! However, you do need to be careful, as the carding is very sharp and will come through the weaver's cloth. After your fabric is stretched in place, cover the carding strips with a thick athletic headband to protect your clothing (and skin) from being snagged.

After stretching the design in the hoop, measure to see that you have stretched the design evenly on all four sides and through the center. If the design is distorted, your finished punched design will also be distorted. Once your weaver's cloth is stretched into position in a hoop or on a stretcher frame, leave it there until you are finished punching. Since you are working from the back of the design, the loops that form on the front will be protected inside the hoop or stretcher frame.

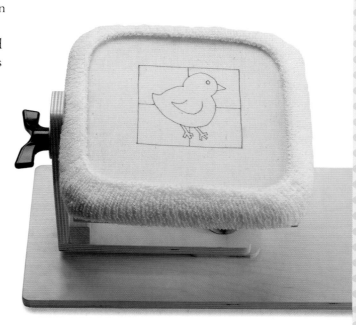

HOW TO PUNCH

Now for the fun part—punching!

Punching on Weaver's Cloth

After properly threading the needle, place the floss over your hand. You don't want to restrict the floss from flowing through the needle in any way. Don't throw the excess floss over your shoulder; the drag from your clothing will cause the loops to become irregular. Hold the needle with your thumb and index finger; then place your middle finger along the side of the needle. Use your hand and little finger on the stretched fabric to aid in controlling the needle. As you punch, move the needle in the direction of the bevel. The bevel indicator will help you see which direction to move your needle. Some needle manufacturers recommend a different direction to drag the bevel. Check the instructions that come with your punchneedle.

The punchneedle stitch is very simple when you learn to control the needle. Practice in an open area to master the stitch.

1. Punch the needle into the fabric until it stops. The gauge prevents the needle from going deeper. Keep the needle perpendicular (or nearly perpendicular) to the fabric.
2. Slowly extract the needle until the tip just clears the fabric.
3. Keeping the tip in contact with the fabric, drag the tip of the needle a short distance to the next stitch. When you learn to control how far the needle comes up out of the fabric, your stitches will become very consistent and smooth across the back of the fabric. If you lift the needle up too far, you will pull out a portion or all of the loop you just made, resulting in an irregular pile.

TIP
To make the CTR punch embroidery needle even more comfortable, place a pencil grip over the handle.

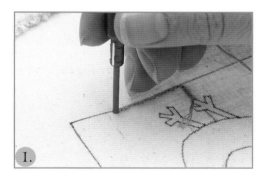

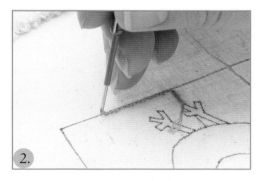

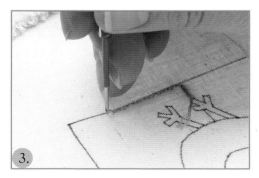

4. Repeat steps I to 3 for several stitches, keeping the bevel turned in the direction of the stitches. Clip the tail of the first stitch even with the background fabric. If your starting stitch makes its way to the front pile, simply cut the longer floss even with the pile.

5. To check your work, leave the needle down in the fabric, and flip the hoop over. The loops should not be packed too tightly; they should be just kissing each other!

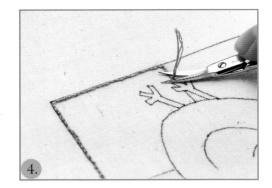

I prefer to punch with a side view of the bevel. If you are right-handed, punch with the bevel traveling from right to left. If you are left-handed, punch with the bevel traveling from left to right. Some people like to punch with the bevel facing toward them. Use the style that feels most comfortable to you; just make sure the bevel always faces the next stitch. When you need to change direction, hold the needle stationary and rotate the hoop, so the bevel stays in the correct direction.

When you work on a design, stitch all the background or lower pile first. I like to outline an area and then fill in to the center. I also like to shadow shapes—echo the outline of a design area. This allows the loops to face many different directions and fill in the area nicely. If you punch too many back and forth rows, the loops will line up in unwanted stripes.

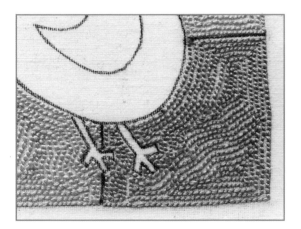
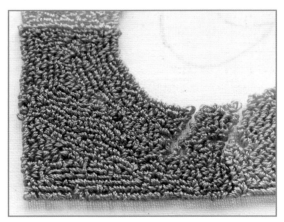

The spacing of the rows and stitches is also important. The length of the stitch is very short. For example, a one-strand stitch length should cross over only one thread in the warp or weft of the fabric. The larger the needle and the more strands of floss used, the longer the stitches should be.

The distance between the rows is about the width of the needle shaft. Overpunching causes the fabric to curl when it is taken out of the hoop and makes framing the design more difficult.

Ending the Floss

When you are stitching, never drag your floss over to an adjacent area or stitch over previously stitched rows. Always stop by cutting the floss and moving the needle to the next section to be stitched. You do not need to tie knots or glue your starting or ending threads.

The cut ends of floss will appear slightly darker in color than the loops. For this reason, some designers pull the ending threads to the back of the design and then cut the floss. I have found that after the floss is cut and the needle is removed, the cut ends slide down below the pile. This is not an issue when you are using overdyed floss, because the variations in the floss hide any change in color that occurs from clipping the floss. I always cut my ending floss from the front. Experiment and decide which method works best for you.

Cutting from the Front

When you have finished using a color or you have worked into the center and are ready to stop, leave the needle down in the fabric. Turn the hoop over to the front. Draw the needle back slightly to allow the floss to come away from the needle shaft. Clip the threads even with the pile of the design. Your needle should remain threaded.

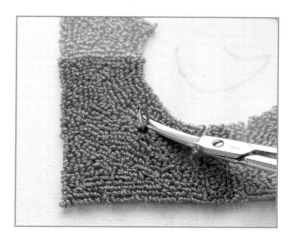

Cutting from the Back

Place your finger on the back of the design, close to the needle. When the needle comes up, place your finger over the floss, and then pull the needle away. Pull the floss away from the tip of the needle, and cut the floss even with the background.

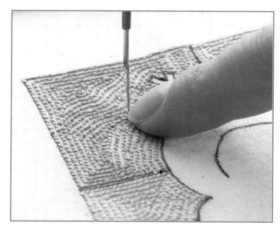

Tips for Success

Here are some hints for avoiding problems.

- Punch the background first. When you add details in a higher pile depth, the longer loops tend to flop over. The background stitches help support them.
- Adjust the gauge by removing or adding one segment from your needle. This varies the loop depths and adds a three-dimensional look to your project.
- When you remove a gauge segment, place it on a safety pin.
- Avoid punching on the drawn lines when filling in the background. If you stay on either side of the lines, you have the perfect spacing for punching in the detail.
- If you get too close to an adjacent row, you risk snagging threads. If that happens, you will feel a slight resistance when punching into the fabric. When you turn the hoop over, one strand of floss will appear higher than all the others. The great thing about punchneedle is how forgiving it is. Just trim the snag even with the pile, and never think about it again!
- Punch detail stitches with a slightly closer spacing. While staying just inside the drawn line, outline and then fill the shape to the center.

- When you make a mistake, simply pull out the undesired stitches. The weave of the fabric will look pulled apart. Just rub the fabric with your finger; the weave will come back into place. Then restitch the area with the new floss.
- Floss removed from a mistake is crinkled and frayed and will not flow well through the needle. Just throw it away.
- If you have worn out an area of the fabric, patch it with a small piece of iron-on woven interfacing, and let it cool to room temperature before punching the area. If you don't have any of the woven interfacing, just cut a small piece of weaver's cloth to place over the worn area. Adjust the gauge to accommodate the thicker fabric.

COLOR EFFECTS AND PILE MANIPULATION

There are various ways to manipulate the threads, stitches, and loops to create interesting textures and color effects in your designs.

Stippling

Thread the needle with overdyed floss. Stitch in an irregular pattern, allowing the color shades to mingle. For example, use one strand of overdyed blue floss that contains four different shades of blue to form a beautiful background by stippling.

BACK

FRONT

Striping the Background

Use an overdyed floss, and stitch back and forth in rows. As the floss changes shades, a striped effect develops.

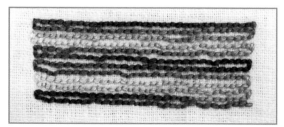

BACK

FRONT

Shading

Cut a skein of overdyed floss into pieces so that one piece begins with the lightest variation of color and another begins with the darkest color. To shade adjacent areas in a design that are the same color, such as flower petals, outline the first area with the lightest color, and fill it to the center. Then outline the next area with the darkest color, and fill it to the center. The areas will stand apart from each other and look naturally shaded.

Color Blending

Thread the needle with three different shades of the same color. For example, combine two light pink colors with one medium pink to stitch a flower with beautifully blended color.

Tweed Background

Thread a three-strand needle with two strands of dark floss and one strand of light floss to stitch a background with a tweed effect. In the same way, thread a six-strand needle with three or four stands of dark floss and two strands of light floss.

Clipping

Floss in the loop pile appears glossy. When you clip the loops, the floss changes dramatically. The sheen disappears, and the color of the floss turns two shades darker. This technique is primarily used to give animals a furry look. It is also great for Santa beards, snow, and anything you want to look fluffy. You can clip loops that are made with a three-strand or six-strand needle, using a gauge of at least ½" (1.3 cm).

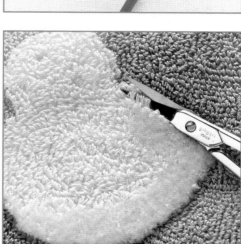

After punching the design, remove the fabric from the hoop. With the pile facing up, roll the fabric over your index finger to separate the loops. Insert the tip of small scissors into each loop, one or several at a time, and cut. Don't worry if you miss a few loops here and there; the different textures really enhance the project.

You may be directed to add details in the design after clipping. For example, you don't want to punch in the eyes, nose, or mouth of an animal until after the face has been clipped, because you risk accidentally clipping the loops that need to stay looped. Remember to place the design back in the hoop, wrong side up.

Shearing

Areas that have been clipped can be sheared and sculpted to give them shape. Clipped loops tend to mingle together, and details can be lost. When you shear off a loop, it stays in place. Use the curvature of the scissor's blades to shear loops into nicely rounded and curved areas. To define an area, shear the loops shorter around the edges. Loops that will be sheared are punched at ⅝" (1.6 cm) gauge measurement.

Raking

Use your needle as a finishing tool. Rake over the loops with the unthreaded tip of the needle to manipulate and fine-tune them. This is especially useful for detailed designs. Raking aligns the loops in their proper position, so stars have crisp points and facial features are more distinct. My design models travel to trunk shows all the time. After a few weeks on the road, a little raking gets them back in shape!

Blocking the Design

After you have finished a design, place it face-up on the ironing board, and press out the crease left from the hoop. Hold the steam iron down on one side of the weaver's cloth as you pull the opposite side of the fabric with your other hand. Push the iron up against the edge of the design, lifting up the outer row of loops. Repeat on all four sides. Do not place the iron on top of the finished design.

PROBLEMS AND SOLUTIONS

Students ask wonderful questions, and the answers always provide an opportunity to learn more. Here are some common problems you may encounter and the ways to solve or prevent them.

PROBLEM: "After I punch, I turn it over, and there are no loops."
SOLUTION: Make sure your needle is threaded properly. Review the steps on page 14. Did you thread the eye of the needle? If your needle is threaded properly, the most common reason for no loop output is restricted thread. I recommend letting the thread drape over your hand so it can feed freely into the handle of the needle. If your thread is dragging on your clothes or is catching around some other object, it won't feed freely into the needle and produce even loops in the fabric.

PROBLEM: "My loops are inconsistent. Some are lower than others."
SOLUTION: Four things can cause this.
1. Lifting the needle off the fabric as you stitch. When you pull up, you should drag the tip of the needle across the fabric and take your next stitch. Lifting the needle too high can pull out a portion of your last loop, causing irregular depths.
2. Punching too shallow. Make sure that you punch down until the gauge contacts the fabric. The gauge is your stopper.
3. Forgetting to hold the needle perpendicular (or nearly perpendicular) to the fabric can also cause irregular loops. Needles vary somewhat. Refer to the directions that came with your needle.
4. Twisting the bevel. You need to stitch with the bevel of the needle leading the stitch. Think of the bevel as the steering wheel of the needle. Again, some needles require different techniques.

PROBLEM: "I have gaps in my pile when I punch."
SOLUTION: Two things can cause this.
1. Check to see if your running stitch is too long. Remember, punchneedle is a short running stitch on the back of the fabric. For every stitch, you should advance your three-strand needle about two or three threads in the weave of the fabric.
2. Restricting the thread can also cause this problem. Any resistance (such as clothing or your finger) can prevent the floss from flowing freely through the needle.

PROBLEM: "When I take my project out of the hoop, it curls up."
SOLUTION: Overpunching causes the project to curl (my first project curled up like a roly-poly!). There should be at least a needle's width between your rows. You can iron the fabric around the project to help it lie flat, but do not iron the project itself.

Steaming from the back might help. Place your design wrong side up on a fluffy white towel. Hover a steam iron slightly above the back of the design for 15 seconds. Repeat if necessary. DO NOT press down with the iron or use bursts of steam because the floss may not be colorfast. Block the design (page 22).

PROBLEM: "I can't help it. I always overpunch."
SOLUTION: Overpunching is very common. Here's one thing that will help. Use two strands of floss in your three-strand needle.

PROBLEM: "I get snags in my pile when I punch."
SOLUTION: Overpunching causes this. If you snag a loop, just cut it off even with the pile depth, and forget it was even there. Don't punch on the lines. This gives you the perfect spacing between the shapes.

PROBLEM: "My thread is jammed in the needle!"
SOLUTION: If you get a knot or thread jam in your needle, don't tear off the floss inside the needle or try to force it through by pulling it out the tip. Gently pull the floss back through the handle. You can also gently work your threader into the tip of the needle, and try to push the thread back through the handle.

FIBER AND FABRIC RECOMMENDATIONS

Many different fibers can be used for punchneedle embroidery, and there is something unique about each of them. Make sure to choose fibers that flow freely through the needle. If the fiber is too thick or textured, it will not produce the desired loops. You can test floss thickness by comparing it to pearl cotton. Size #12 pearl cotton is suitable for the one-strand needle; size #8 is suitable for the three-strand needle; and size #5 is suitable for the six-strand needle.

Here are some of the fibers and fabrics that I enjoy using in my designs.

DMC Fibers
465 colors of Mouline six-ply cotton embroidery floss and pearl cotton in sizes #12, #8, and #5.

Use with these needles:
one-strand: pearl cotton size #12
three-strand: pearl cotton size #8
six-strand: pearl cotton size #5
Available at craft or needlework stores.

Presencia Hilatura Fibers
Finca Mouline, 100 percent mercerized Egyptian cotton six-ply embroidery floss and pearl cotton in sizes #12, #8, and #5.

Use with these needles:
one-strand: pearl cotton size #12
three-strand: pearl cotton size #8
six-strand: pearl cotton size #5
Available at needlework or quilt stores.

The Caron Collection Ltd.
Wildflowers is a single-strand hand-dyed cotton in variegated colors. It is between a size #8 and size #12 pearl cotton in weight—equivalent to two strands of other brands of floss. You won't

need to separate this floss to use in your three-strand punchneedle; just space your rows a little closer together.

Impressions is a 50 percent wool, 50 percent silk blend. It comes in solid colors and hand-dyed colors. The blend of wool and silk works great in your three- or six-strand punchneedle.

Snow is an opalescent synthetic thread. It is similar to size #5 pearl cotton or six strands of floss. The sparkle is beautiful when used in your six-strand punchneedle.

Visit www.caron-net.com.

Dream House Ventures, Inc.

Soy Luster solids and shadows are 100 percent Soy Silk and formaldehyde free. They have 82 delicious colors that contain 36 continuous yards (33 m). Use this silk floss in a one-strand punchneedle or in the three-strand punchneedle.

Visit www.thepurepalatte.com.

TIP
Wind the 36 yards (33 m) of Soy Luster floss on a spool. You can keep punching for a long time as it feeds off the spool.

The Gentle Art

This company produces "gently" overdyed, six-ply cotton embroidery floss called Sampler Threads. It is beautiful floss with a primitive appearance, available in five-yard (4.6 m) and ten-yard (9.15 m) skeins that are precut in one-yard (0.92 m) lengths.

Use them in one-, three-, and six-strand punchneedles.

Visit www.thegentleart.com.

Gloriana Threads

Gloriana Lorikeet is an overdyed, nine-ply, 100 percent Australian wool. It may be plied down to one strand to fit in your three-strand punchneedle. I love the subtle shades of color and the soft appearance it gives to the design. See Crossed Tulips on page 60.

Visit www.glorianathreads.com.

Weeks Dye Works

Over 200 colors of hand-overdyed six-ply cotton embroidery floss. The colors are variegated enough to be noticeable, yet subtle enough to blend naturally. This floss is perfect for one-, three-, and six-strand punchneedles. Each skein contains five yards (4.6 m) in a continuous length.

150 hand-dyed pearl cotton colors in size #8 for the three-strand punchneedle and size #5 for the six-strand punchneedle. Each skein contains ten yards (9.15 m) in a continuous length.

Visit www.weeksdyeworks.com.

Weeks Dye Works 100 percent hand-dyed wool fabric is colorfast, felted, and great for wool appliqué, penny rugs, and rug hooking. It is also perfect for pillows, purses, clothing, and finishing for punchneedle. Wool with HTC Form Flex Interfacing can also be used for punchneedle. They offer each color in three patterns: solid, houndstooth, and herringbone. I love using it to accent my punchneedle patterns. Their hand-dyed cotton flosses coordinate with their hand-dyed wools. (See the wool-framed piggy on page 68.)

Weeks Dye Works weaver's cloth collection currently features ten hand-dyed colors. With a colored background, this hand-dyed weaver's cloth makes finishing your punchneedle pieces much easier. (See page 72. "Summer Through My Window" has been mounted on foam core board and framed.)

Nordic Gold by Rainbow Gallery

Nordic Gold is a very fine chainette knit metallic that is excellent for the three-strand punch-needle. Because it is so flexible, the metallic punches into the fabric and looks just like tinsel. Nordic Gold comes in sixteen colors and works best when used with a 1/2" (1.3 cm) gauge setting.

Valdani Inc.

The original creator of 3-Strand Floss™, Valdani has 180 hand-overdyed, colorfast flosses for the three-strand punchneedle. The balls are 29 or 88 continuous yards (26.7 or 81 m) and the spools come in 88 continuous yards (81 m). More fun, less work! New colors are being added monthly with a target of 300 colors.

130 hand-overdyed, colorfast colors of six-strand floss, including subtle-shaded colors and subdued variegates.

400 colors of hand-overdyed, colorfast pearl cotton in size 5, 8, and 12. They come in several fabulous designer collections. Use the size 5 in your six-strand, size 8 in your three-strand and size 12 in your one-strand.

Visit www.valdani.com to order and see the different designer color collections.

PROJECTS

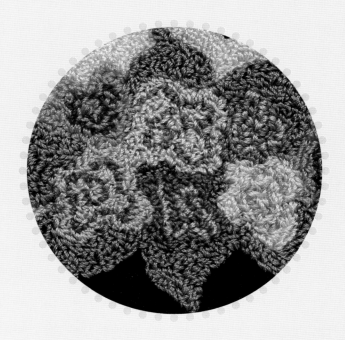

Duncan

I was invited to teach at a needlework shop called
"Dyeing to Stitch" in Virginia Beach, VA.
While I was there, I met their adorable Scottish terrier.
"Duncan" reminds me of that wonderful visit.

Not to scale. Actual size is 4¼" x 4" (10.8 x 10.2 cm).

1. Trace the pattern to the weaver's cloth. Place the design so that the weft of the fabric is vertical and the warp is horizontal. (See diagram.)

2. Place the fabric in the hoop or frame with the design facing up. Make sure the fabric is pulled drum tight. You will be working from the back to the front.

3. Adjust the needle for a ⅜" (1 cm) gauge. Punch areas 1, 2, and 3 in order. Refer to the numbered chart for the placement of each color.

4. Adjust the needle for a ½" (1.3 cm) gauge. Punch areas 4 to 8 in order. Refer to the numbered chart for the placement of each color.

5. Remove the design from the hoop. Clip the loops (page 21) on the thistle top. Sculpt the thistle by trimming the threads shorter on the outside edges, leaving the center longer. Rub your finger over the clipped loops to fluff them up.

Materials

three-strand punchneedle
weaver's cloth (natural)
3½" (8.9 cm) curved-tip scissors
7" (17.8 cm) hoop

DMC Floss:
310 black (2), 334 blue, 3363 green,
3608 bright pink

Weeks Dye Works Floss:
2223 Saffron (4) and 4135 Foliage

Substitutions:
DMC 725 (2) for WDW Saffron
DMC 346 and 3022 (mixed)
   for WDW Foliage

1	WDW 2223 Saffron	5	WDW 4135 Foliage
2	DMC 310 Black (Punch directly on the line)	6	DMC 3608 bright pink
3	DMC 334 blue	7	DMC 310 black
4	DMC 3363 green	8	DMC 334 blue

This Little Piggy

Unlike most pigs, this little guy is clean and cute.

And, he wants to come live in your house.

Not to scale. Actual size is 3⅝" x 3½" (9.2 x 8.9 cm).

1. Trace the pattern to the weaver's cloth. Place the design so that the weft of the fabric is vertical and the warp is horizontal. (See diagram.)

2. Place the fabric in the hoop or frame with the design facing up. Make sure the fabric is pulled drum tight. You will be working from the back to the front.

3. Separate the six-strand floss into two three-strand units.

4. Adjust the needle for a ⅜" (1 cm) gauge. Punch areas 1 to 8 in order. Refer to the numbered chart for the placement of each color.

   Optional: After punching areas 1 to 4, adjust the needle for a ½" (1.3 cm) gauge. Punch areas 5 to 8 in order. Refer to the numbered chart for the placement of each color.

5. Rake the loops (page 22) into place for a nice sharp image.

Materials

three-strand punchneedle
weaver's cloth
3½" (8.9 cm) curved-tip scissors
6" (15.2 cm) hoop

DMC Floss:
209 purple, 310 black,
335 dark pink, 743 bright yellow,
800 blue, 818 light pink,
954 light green

1 DMC 743 bright yellow	6 DMC 310 black
2 DMC 954 light green	7 DMC 335 dark pink
3 DMC 800 light blue	8 Outline the pig with
4 DMC 209 purple	DMC 335 dark pink
5 DMC 818 light pink	(Punch directly on the lines.)

Baa, Baa, Black Sheep

I may be the black sheep of the family,
but I'm an adorable addition to any nursery.

Not to scale. Actual size is 4⅛" x 4" (10.5 x 10.2 cm) with border.

1. Trace the pattern to the weaver's cloth. Place the design so that the weft of the fabric is vertical and the warp is horizontal. (See diagram.)

2. Place the fabric in the hoop or frame with the design facing up. Make sure the fabric is pulled drum tight. You will be working from the back to the front.

3. Separate the six-strand floss into two three-strand units.

4. Adjust the needle for a ⅜" (1 cm) gauge. Punch areas 1 to 9 in order. Refer to the numbered chart for the placement of each color.

   Optional: After punching areas 1 to 6, adjust the needle for a ½" (1.3 cm) gauge. Punch areas 7 to 9 in order. Refer to the numbered chart for the placement of each color.

   Optional: Make a border around the design with Wildflower by Caron 086 Tahiti. Do not separate this floss. (I went around the design four times.)

5. Rake the loops (page 22) into place for a nice sharp image.

Materials

three-strand punchneedle
weaver's cloth
3½" (8.9 cm) curved-tip scissors
6" (15.2 cm) hoop

DMC Floss:

Blanc (white), 310 black,
743 bright yellow, 800 blue,
954 light green, 3045 tan, 3716 pink

Optional:

Impressions by Caron 000 White
   (body of sheep)

Optional border:

Wildflower by Caron
   086 Tahiti

1. DMC 954 light green
2. DMC 800 blue
3. DMC 743 bright orange
4. DMC 3716 pink
5. DMC 3045 tan
6. DMC 310 black
7. DMC Blanc (white)
   (Optional: Impressions by
   Caron 000 Wool/Silk Blend)
8. DMC 310 black
9. DMC Blanc (white)
   (Optional: Impressions by
   Caron 000 Wool/Silk Blend)
10. Optional border:
    Wildflowers 086 Tahiti

Peep, Peep

When I see a baby chick, I can't help thinking of all the
Easter egg hunts we experienced with our daughter, Laura.
Along with the colored real eggs, we would hide large plastic eggs.
Inside those large eggs were tiny stuffed animals and
other treasures. I will never forget the look on her face
when she discovered a toy baby chick inside.

Not to scale. Actual size is 3⅝" x 3½" (9.2 x 8.9 cm).

1. Trace the pattern to the weaver's cloth. Place the design so that the weft of the fabric is vertical and the warp is horizontal. (See diagram.)

2. Place the fabric in the hoop or frame with the design facing up. Make sure the fabric is pulled drum tight. You will be working from the back to the front.

3. Separate the six-strand floss into two three-strand units.

4. Adjust the needle for a ⅜" (1 cm) gauge. Punch areas 1 to 5 in order. Refer to the numbered chart for the placement of color.

5. Adjust the needle for a ½" (1.3 cm) gauge. Punch area 6.

6. Remove the design from the hoop. Clip the loops (page 21) on the entire chick. Rub your finger over the clipped loops to fluff them up.

7. Place the pattern back into the hoop wrong side up. Punch area 7 and 8.

8. Adjust the needle for a ⅝" (1.6 cm) gauge. You will have a very high loop that will come up above the clipped chick. Punch area 9 to outline and on the inside line to form the wing.

9. Shear off the loops (page 22) of the wing following this method: Place the scissors even with the clipped chick. "Shear off" the loops by cutting them even with the clipped loops.

10. Hold your scissors at a 45-degree angle, and shear off the loops to outline the chick. Also shear off some of the chick's body to give the outside edge a three-dimensional look. Be very careful when shearing off the loops across the beak. Shear the loops off even with the beak.

11. Rake the loops (page 22) into place for a nice sharp image.

Materials

three-strand punchneedle
weaver's cloth (natural)
3½" (8.9 cm) inch curved-tip scissors
6" (15.2 cm) hoop

DMC Floss:
209 purple, 310 black,
743 light orange, 800 blue,
954 green, 3078 pale yellow,
3716 pink

1 DMC 800 blue	6	DMC 3078 pale yellow
2 DMC 3716 pink	7	DMC 310 black
3 DMC 954 green	8	DMC 743 light orange, beak
4 DMC 209 purple	9	DMC 743 light orange
5 DMC 743 light orange		(Outline the chick and punch on the line for the wing.)

Westie on Alert

I couldn't design a pattern for a Scottish terrier without designing a pattern for a West Highland terrier. I dedicate this design to the West Highland terriers that have warmed my heart: Truman, Daisy, McDuff, and Hayden.

Not to scale. Actual size is 4¼" X 4" (10.8 X 10.2 cm).

1. Trace the pattern to the weaver's cloth. Place the design so that the weft of the fabric is vertical and the warp is horizontal. (See diagram.)

2. Place the fabric in the hoop or frame with the design facing up. Make sure the fabric is pulled drum tight. You will be working from the back to the front.

3. Separate the six-strand floss into two three-strand units.

4. Adjust the needle for a ⅜" (1 cm) gauge. Punch areas 1 to 3 in order. Refer to the numbered chart for the placement of each color.

5. Adjust the needle for a ½" (1.3 cm) gauge. Punch areas 4 to 7 in order. Refer to the numbered chart for the placement of each color.

6. Remove the design from the hoop. Clip the loops (page 21) on the West Highland terrier. Hold your scissors at a 45-degree angle, and sculpt the dog by trimming the threads shorter on the outside edges, leaving the center longer. Rub your finger over the clipped loops to fluff them up.

7. Place the design back into the hoop wrong side up. Punch areas 8 and 9.

8. Rake the loops (page 22) into place for a nice sharp image.

Materials

three-strand punchneedle
weaver's cloth
3½" (8.9 cm) curved-tip scissors
8" (20.3 cm) hoop

DMC Floss:
Blanc (white), 310 black, 321 red,
905 bright green

Weeks Dye Works Floss:
2333 Peoria Purple, 2223 Saffron,
2226 Carrot

Substitutions:
DMC 333 for WDW Peoria Purple
DMC 725 for WDW Saffron
DMC 922 for WDW Carrot

1. WDW 2333 Peoria Purple
2. DMC 321 red,
   line between the two backgrounds
3. DMC 310 black
4. DMC Blanc (white)
5. WDW 2223 Saffron
6. WDW 2226 Carrot,
   lines inside the flowers
7. DMC 905 bright green
8. DMC 321 red
9. DMC 310 black

Bunny

Everyone loves an adorable bunny!

This little guy likes to be shown off on a shirt, especially around Easter.

Not to scale. Actual size is 1½" x 1½" (3.8 x 3.8 cm).

1. Trace the pattern to the weaver's cloth. Place the design so that the weft of the fabric is horizontal and the warp is vertical. (See diagram.)

2. Place the fabric in the hoop or frame with the design facing up. Make sure the fabric is pulled drum tight. You will be working from the back to the front.

3. Separate the six-strand floss into two three-strand units.

4. Adjust the needle for a ⅜" (1cm) gauge. Punch area 1 for the background. Refer to the numbered chart for the placement of each color.

5. Adjust the needle for a ½" (1.3 cm) gauge. Punch areas 2 to 4.

6. Remove the design from the hoop. Clip the loops (page 21) on the entire bunny. Hold your scissors at a 45-degree angle, and sculpt the bunny by trimming the threads shorter on the outside edges, leaving the center longer. Rub your finger over the clipped loops to fluff them up.

7. Place the pattern back into the hoop wrong side up. Punch areas 5 to 7.

8. Adjust the needle for a ⅝" (1.6 cm) gauge. You will have a very high loop that will come up above the clipped bunny. Punch area 8 on the line.

9. Shear off the loops of the mouth (page 22) even with the clipped bunny.

10. Rake the loops (page 22) into place for a nice sharp image.

TIP

Make the eyes by punching three times around the circle with white, then two punches into the center with black. Cut from the front after the second punch.

Materials

three-strand punchneedle
weaver's cloth
3½" (8.9 cm) curved-tip scissors
5" (12.7 cm) hoop

DMC Floss:

Blanc (white), 310 black,
335 dark pink, 818 pink,

Weeks Dye Works Floss:

4111 Lucky

Substitution:

DMC 3347 and 3362 (mixed)
   for WDW Lucky

1	WDW 4111 Lucky	5	DMC 335 dark pink
2	DMC 310 black	6	DMC Blanc (white)
3	DMC Blanc (white)	7	DMC 310 black
4	DMC 818 pink	8	DMC 310 black

This Is Not a Partridge

I designed this pattern just because I love red birds.

Everyone who sees it automatically says,

"Oh, a partridge in a pear tree."

But this is not a partridge; it's just a pretty bird!

Not to scale. Actual size is 3¾" x 3¾" (9.5 x 9.5 cm).

1. Trace the pattern to the weaver's cloth. Place the design so that the weft of the fabric is horizontal and the warp is vertical. (See diagram.)

2. Place the fabric in the hoop or frame with the design facing up. Make sure the fabric is pulled drum tight. You will be working from the back to the front.

3. Separate the six-strand floss into two three-strand units.

4. Adjust the needle for a ⅜" (1 cm) gauge. Punch areas 1 to 11 in order. Refer to the numbered chart for the placement of each color.

5. Rake the loops (page 22) into place for a nice sharp image.

Materials

three-strand punchneedle
weaver's cloth
3½" (8.9 cm) curved-tip scissors
6" (15.2 cm) hoop

DMC Floss:

310 black, 817 orange/red, 400 rust,
433 brown, 677 yellow, 498 dark red,
905 green, 677 light yellow,
733 yellow/green,
734 light yellow/green,
739 cream, 934 dark green,
3755 blue

1 DMC 3755 blue
2 DMC 433 brown
3 DMC 934 dark green
4 DMC 934; two strands mixed with one strand of DMC 905 green
5 DMC 739 cream
6 DMC 817 orange/red
7 DMC 498 dark red, and outline the middle tail feather
8 DMC 400 rust
9 DMC 310 black
10 DMC 733 yellow/green
11 Two strands of DMC 677 yellow mixed with one strand of DMC 734 light yellow/green

Blooming Heart

Simple and versatile, this pretty project can be finished numerous ways. Make a purse, an eyeglass case, or a chatelaine to hold your needlework accessories.

Not to scale. Actual size is 3¼" x 5" (8.3 x 12.7 cm).

NOTE: Do not use Form Flex if you are using the Linen weaver's cloth. It will not need to be stabilized. One hundred percent cotton fabric is not as durable as weaver's cloth.

1. Trace the pattern to the weaver's cloth. Place the design so that the weft of the fabric is vertical and the warp is horizontal. (See diagram.)

2. Place the fabric in the hoop or frame with the design facing up. Make sure the fabric is pulled drum tight. You will be working from the back to the front.

3. Separate the six-strand floss into two three-strand units.

4. Adjust the needle for a ⅜" (1 cm) gauge. Punch areas 1 to 4 in order. Refer to the numbered chart for the placement of each color.

5. Rake the loops (page 22) into place for a nice sharp image.

Materials

three-strand punchneedle
weaver's cloth (WDW 1094 Linen)
Or woven interfacing (HTC Form Flex)
  for use with 100 percent
  cotton fabrics
3½" (8.9 cm) curved-tip scissors
8" (20.3 cm) hoop

DMC Floss:
335 pink, 816 (2) red,
905 green

1	DMC 816 red	3	DMC 335 pink
2	DMC 905 green	4	DMC 816 red

Spring Through My Window

As nature reawakens, beautiful new flowers emerge
and the birds are everywhere.
The fragrance is wonderful, and the view from my window
lifts my spirit.

Not to scale. Actual size is 3½" x 5¾" (8.9 x 14.6 cm).

1. Trace the pattern to the weaver's cloth. Place the design so that the weft of the fabric is horizontal and the warp is vertical. (See diagram.)

2. Place the fabric in the hoop or frame with the design facing up. Make sure the fabric is pulled drum tight. You will be working from the back to the front.

3. Separate the six-strand floss into two three-strand units.

4. Adjust the needle for a ⅜" (1 cm) gauge. Punch areas 1 to 7 in order. Refer to the numbered chart for the placement of each color.

5. Adjust the needle for a ½" (1.3 cm) gauge. Punch areas 8 to 17 in order.

6. Rake the loops (page 22) into place for a nice sharp image.

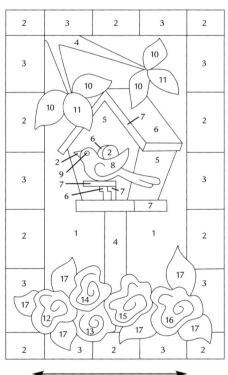

Materials

three-strand punchneedle
weaver's cloth
  (WDW 2109 Morris Blue)
3½" (8.9 cm) curved-tip scissors
8" (20.3 cm) hoop

DMC Floss:

Blanc (white), 211 lavender,
309 black, 310 black, 347 red,
  433 medium brown,
436 dark tan,
500 dark green,
552 purple, 605 pink,
742 orange, 826 blue,
898 brown, 922 medium orange,
3350 dark pink

Weeks Dye Works Floss:

2109 Morris Blue,
1115 Banana Popsicle,
4111 Lucky

Substitutions:

DMC 162 for WDW Morris Blue
DMC 743 and 746 (mixed) for
  WDW Banana Popsicle
DMC 3347 and 3362 (mixed)
  for WDW Lucky

1 WDW 2109 Morris Blue

2 DMC Blanc (white)

3 DMC 310 black
  (You will also fill in the birdhouse hole and bird's beak.)

4 DMC 898 brown

5 WDW 1115 Banana Popsicle

6 DMC 433 medium brown
  (rooftop, perch, outline for the birdhouse)

7 DMC 436 dark tan

8 DMC 347 red

9 Line under the wing and eye DMC 310 black

10 DMC 500 dark green

11 WDW 4111 Lucky

12 DMC 605 pink
  (Punch on the inside lines with DMC 3350 dark pink.)

13 DMC 826 blue
  (Punch on the inside lines with DMC 742 orange.)

14 DMC 742 orange
  (Punch on the inside lines with DMC medium orange.)

15 DMC 3350 dark pink
  (Punch on the lines with with DMC 605 pink.)

16 DMC 552 purple
  (Punch on the inside lines with DMC 211 lavender.)

17 WDW 4111 Lucky

Summer Through My Window

We love the outdoors in summer. One thing I have
never mastered is how to pick a good watermelon.
Thankfully, my parents live nearby. I can always depend on
my mom to bring over the sweetest one of them all.
Thanks mom, you can always make me smile!

Not to scale. Actual size is 3½" x 5¾" (8.9 x 14.6 cm).

1. Trace the pattern to the weaver's cloth. Place the design so that the weft of the fabric is horizontal and the warp is vertical. (See diagram.)

2. Place the fabric in the hoop or frame with the design facing up. Make sure the fabric is pulled drum tight. You will be working from the back to the front.

3. Separate the six-strand floss into two three-strand units.

4. Adjust the needle for a ⅜" (1 cm) gauge. Punch areas 1 to 9 in order. Refer to the numbered chart for the placement of each color.

5. Adjust the needle for a ½" (1.3 cm) gauge. Punch areas 10 to 17 in order.

6. Rake the loops (page 22) into place for a nice sharp image.

Materials

three-strand punchneedle
weaver's cloth
  (WDW 2109 Morris Blue)
3½" (8.9 cm) curved-tip scissors
8" (20.3 cm) hoop

DMC Floss:
Blanc (white), 310 black,
311 dark blue, 433 medium brown,
436 dark tan,
500 dark green,
826 blue, 898 brown,
3350 dark pink, 905 green

Weeks Dye Works floss:
109 Morris Blue,
1115 Banana Popsicle,
2203 Chartreuse, 4111 Lucky

Weeks Dye Works Floss:
2109 Morris Blue,
1115 Banana Popsicle, 4111 Lucky

Substitutions:
DMC 162 for WDW Morris Blue
DMC 743 and 746 (mixed) for
  WDW Banana Popsicle
DMC 3347 and 3362 (mixed)
  for WDW Lucky

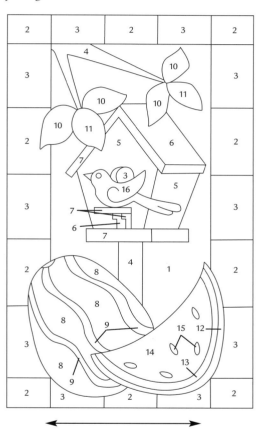

1 WDW 2109 Morris Blue
2 DMC Blanc (white)
3 DMC 310 black
   (You will also fill in the birdhouse hole and bird's beak.)
4 DMC 898 brown
5 WDW 1115 Banana Popsicle
6 DMC 433 medium brown
   (rooftop, perch, outline for the birdhouse)
7 DMC 436 dark tan
8 WDW 4111 Lucky
9 WDW 2203 Chartreuse
10 DMC 500 dark green
11 WDW 4111 Lucky
12 DMC 905 green, outside rind
13 DMC Blanc (white), inside rind
14 DMC 3350 dark pink, watermelon slice
15 DMC 310 black, seeds
16 DMC 826 blue, outline with DMC 311 dark blue
17 DMC 310 black, eye

Fall Through My Window

Images of autumn bring memories of Halloween
and Thanksgiving.

How about a slice of pumpkin pie?

Not to scale. Actual size is 3½" x 5¾" (8.9 x 14.6 cm).

1. Trace the pattern to the weaver's cloth. Place the design so that the weft of the fabric is horizontal and the warp is vertical. (See diagram.)

2. Place the fabric in the hoop or frame with the design facing up. Make sure the fabric is pulled drum tight. You will be working from the back to the front.

3. Separate the six-strand floss into two three-strand units.

4. Adjust the needle for a ⅜" (1 cm) gauge. Punch areas 1 to 11 in order. Refer to the numbered chart for the placement of each color.

5. Adjust the needle for a ½" (1.3 cm) gauge. Punch areas 12 to 20 in order.

6. Rake the loops (page 22) into place for a nice sharp image.

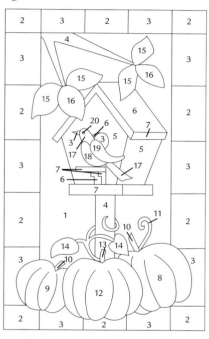

Materials

three-strand punchneedle
weaver's cloth
 (WDW 2109 Morris Blue)
3½" (8.9 cm) curved-tip scissors
8" (20.3 cm) hoop

DMC Floss:
Blanc (white), 300 rust, 310 black,
347 orange/red,

433 medium brown,

436 dark tan, 898 brown,

905 green, 918 burnt orange,

920 dark orange, 921 orange,

976 light orange, 3371 dark brown,

3777 rusty red, 3826 orange/brown,

3827 pale orange, 3829 gold

Weeks Dye Works Floss:
2109 Morris Blue,
1115 Banana Popsicle

Substitutions:
DMC 162 for
 WDW Morris Blue
DMC 743 and 746 (mixed) for
 WDW Banana Popsicle

1 WDW 2109 Morris Blue
2 DMC Blanc (white)
3 DMC 310 black
 (You will also fill in the bird's beak and birdhouse hole.)
4 DMC 898 brown
5 WDW 1115 Banana Popsicle
6 DMC 433 medium brown
 (rooftop, perch, and outline for the birdhouse)
7 DMC 436 dark tan
8 DMC 3826 orange/brown and outline with DMC 918 burnt orange, large pumpkin
9 DMC 920 dark orange and outline with DMC 976 light orange, small pumpkin
10 DMC 3829 gold, stem

11 DMC 905 green, vine
12 DMC 3827 pale orange and outline with DMC 921 orange, middle pumpkin
13 DMC 3829 gold, stem
14 DMC 905 green, leaves and vine
15 DMC 3777 rusty red, tree leaves
16 Mix one strand 3829 gold with two strands 921 orange, tree leaves
17 Mix one strand 3371 dark brown with two strands of 300 rust, birds head and tail
18 DMC 347 orange/red, bird's chest
19 DMC 3371 dark brown, bird's wing
20 Eye: DMC436 dark tan (Punch in between the rows to form the eye.)

Winter Through My Window

A happy snowman presides over his winter domain.
Although we don't see many snowmen in Texas,
occasionally through my window I can see dormant trees
covered with snow. It makes me feel warm inside.

Not to scale. Actual size is 3½" x 5¾" (8.9 x 14.6 cm).

1. Trace the pattern to the weaver's cloth. Place the design so that the weft of the fabric is horizontal and the warp is vertical. (See diagram.)

2. Place the fabric in the hoop or frame with the design facing up. Make sure the fabric is pulled drum tight. You will be working from the back to the front.

3. Separate the six-strand floss into two three-strand units.

4. Adjust the needle for a ⅜" (1 cm) gauge. Punch areas 1 to 8 in order. Refer to the chart.

5. Adjust the needle for a ½" (1.3 cm) gauge. Punch areas 9 to 13 in order.

6. Remove the design from the hoop. Clip the loops (page 21) on the snowman and sculpt the shape.

7. Place the pattern back into the hoop wrong side up. Punch areas 14 to 17 in order.

8. Adjust the needle for a 1¼" (3.2 cm) gauge (all gauge segments will be removed). Punch area 18. Punch the long loops in one straight line across the ends of the scarf.

9. Rake the loops (page 22) into place for a nice sharp image.

Materials

three-strand punchneedle
weaver's cloth (WDW 2109
   Morris Blue)
3½" (8.9 cm) curved-tip scissors
8" (20.3 cm) hoop

DMC Floss:
   Blanc (white), 310 black,
      321 red,
433 medium brown,
436 dark tan, 815 medium red,
898 brown, 3776 medium orange

Weeks Dye Works Floss:
2109 Morris Blue,
1115 Banana Popsicle,
4125 Snowflake

Rainbow Gallery Floss:
Nordic Gold ND 5 Purple Metallic

Substitutions:
DMC 162 for WDW Morris Blue
DMC 743 and 746 (mixed) for
   WDW Banana Popsicle
DMC B5200 for WDW
   Snowflake

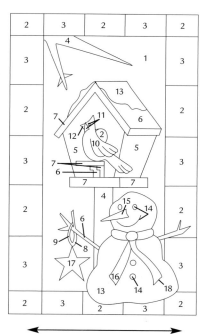

1 WDW 2109 Morris Blue
2 DMC Blanc (white)
3 DMC 310 black
   (You will also fill in the birdhouse hole.)
4 DMC 898 brown
5 WDW 1115 Banana Popsicle
6 DMC 433 medium brown
   (rooftop, perch, outline for the birdhouse and snowman's arms)
7 DMC 436 dark tan
8 DMC 321 red
   (back of the ornament string)
9 DMC 321 red
   (front of the ornament string)
10 DMC 321 red and outline
   with DMC 815 medium red
11 310 black
   (face on the cardinal and eye)
12 DMC 3776 medium orange
13 WDW 4125 Snowflake
14 DMC 310 black
   (eyes, mouth, and buttons)
15 DMC 3776 medium orange
16 Mix two strands of DMC 321 red
   with one strand DMC 310 black
17 ND 5 Purple Metallic
   (This metallic floss will punch in like tinsel.)
18 Mix two strands of DMC 321 red
   with one strand DMC 310 black

Bless Our Home

Literally a stitch and a prayer,

this traditional piece

is perfect for any home.

Give it as a gift or keep it for yourself.

Not to scale. Actual size is 4⅛" x 4⅛" (10.5 x 10.5 cm).

1. Trace the pattern to the weaver's cloth. Place the design so that the weft of the fabric is horizontal and the warp is vertical. (See diagram.)

2. Place the fabric in the hoop or frame with the design facing up. Make sure the fabric is pulled drum tight. You will be working from the back to the front.

3. Separate the six-strand floss into two three-strand units.

4. Adjust the needle for a ⅜" (1 cm) gauge. Punch areas 1 and 2 in order.

5. Adjust the needle for a ½" (1.3 cm) gauge. Punch areas 3 to 5 in order. Refer to the numbered chart for the placement of each color.

6. Rake the loops (page 22) into place for a nice sharp image.

Materials

three-strand punchneedle
weaver's cloth
3½" (8.9 cm) curved-tip scissors
7" (17.8 cm) hoop

DMC Floss:
676 (3) yellow/gold, 902 burgundy,
806 blue, 917 dark pink,
988 green

1	DMC 676 yellow/gold	4	DMC 902 burgundy
2	DMC 806 blue, lettering and outside border	5	DMC 988 green, stems and leaves
3	DMC 917 dark pink		

Guardian Angel

Do you ever wonder if you have a guardian angel?

Well, now you do!

Not to scale. Actual size is 3⅞" x 4" (9.9 x 10.2 cm).

1. Trace the pattern to the weaver's cloth. Place the design so that the weft of the fabric is horizontal and the warp is vertical. (See diagram.)

2. Place the fabric in the hoop or frame with the design facing up. Make sure the fabric is pulled drum tight. You will be working from the back to the front.

3. Separate the six-strand floss into two three-strand units.

4. Adjust the needle for a ⅜" (1 cm) gauge. Punch areas 1 to 7 in order. Refer to the numbered chart for the placement of each color.

5. Adjust the needle for a ½" (1.3 cm) gauge. Punch areas 8 to 17 in order.

6. Rake the loops (page 22) into place for a nice sharp image.

Materials

three-strand punchneedle
weaver's cloth (natural)
3½" (8.9 cm) curved-tip scissors
7" (17.8 cm) hoop

DMC Floss:

Blanc (white), 310 black,
311 dark blue, 326 dark pink,
712 cream, 725 yellow, 818 light pink,
826 medium blue, 869 brown,
962 pink

1 DMC 311 dark blue

2 DMC Blanc (white)
   (line between 311 dark blue
   and 826 medium blue)

3 DMC 826 medium blue

4 DMC 725 yellow (stars and
   swirls in the background)

5 DMC 712 cream (legs)

6 DMC 326 dark pink (socks)

7 DMC 310 black (shoes)

8 DMC Blanc (white)
   (top of the dress)

9 DMC 326 dark pink (dress,
   collar, buttons, and outline
   around the arms)

10 DMC Blanc (white) (line on
    the bottom of the dress)

11 DMC 712 cream
    (face and hands)

12 DMC 869 brown (hair and
    outline around the hands)

13 DMC 725 yellow (large star)

14 DMC 310 black (eyes)

15 DMC 962 pink (mouth)

16 DMC 818 light pink (wings;
    do not punch on the lines)

17 DMC 962 pink (lines inside
    the wings and outline around
    the wings)

Laura

I was reading an article on antique silhouettes, looked up
and saw my daughter's silhouette hanging on the wall.
This is the silhouette of my daughter, Laura.
I made it when she was in second grade.
Customize this pattern with a special child in your life.

Not to scale. Actual size is 4¼" x 4½" (10.8 x 11.4 cm).

1. Draw a silhouette of a child. Reduce the silhouette to fit in the 3½" x 2¾" (8.9 x 7 cm) opening.

2. Trace only the border design on the weaver's cloth if you want to use your own silhouette. Make sure the weft of the fabric is horizontal and the warp is vertical. (See diagram.)

3. Place the fabric in the hoop or frame with the drawn border facing down. This will allow you to trace the design with the fabric flat against the light box or sunny window. Make sure the fabric is pulled drum tight.

4. Place the silhouette on a light box or tape it to a sunny window.

5. Place the hoop so that you can trace the silhouette inside the space. You will be working on the same side as the drawn border. You need to trace the silhouette in the space when it is pulled drum tight. Otherwise the head shape will become distorted.

6. Take the fabric out of the hoop. Place it back in the hoop with the design facing up. Make sure the fabric is pulled drum tight.

7. Separate the six-strand floss into two three-strand units.

8. Adjust the needle for a ⅜" (1 cm) gauge. Punch areas 1 to 4 in order. Refer to the numbered chart for the placement of each color.

TIP
To get a real sharp line around the face, punch the first two rows close together. Continue the rest of the rows with the correct spacing. Remember, you need to see the background fabric between the rows.

Materials

three-strand punchneedle
weaver's cloth
3½" (8.9 cm) curved-tip scissors
7" (17.8 cm) hoop
light box, optional

DMC Floss:
310 black, 676 yellow

1 DMC 676 yellow,
   silhouette background
2 DMC 310 black, silhouette
3 DMC 310 black,
   border background
4 DMC 676 yellow, vines

Bouquet of Flowers

There's nothing like a beautiful basket of fresh flowers
to brighten your day. You'll enjoy creating this
lovely still life painted with thread.

Not to scale. Actual size is 5" x 5" (12.7 x 12.7 cm).

1. Trace the pattern to the weaver's cloth. Place the design so that the weft of the fabric is vertical and the warp is horizontal. (See diagram.)

2. Place the fabric in the hoop or frame with the design facing up. Make sure the fabric is pulled drum tight. You will be working from the back to the front.

3. Separate the six-strand floss into two three-strand units.

4. Adjust the needle for a ⅜" (1 cm) gauge. Punch areas 1 and 2 in order.

5. Adjust the needle for a ½" (1.3 cm) gauge. Punch areas 3 to 10 in order. Refer to the numbered chart for the placement of each color.

6. Rake the loops (page 22) into place for a nice sharp image.

Materials

three-strand punchneedle
weaver's cloth (natural)
8" (20.3 cm) hoop
3½" (8.9 cm) curved-tip scissors

DMC Floss:

310 black, 335 dark pink, 553 purple,
743 yellow, 800 light blue, 815 dark red,
817 dark red, 826 dark blue,
919 dark orange, 922 light orange,
988 green, 3326 pink,
3853 bright orange

Weeks Dye Works:

1115 Banana Popsicle (3)

Substitution:

DMC 743 and 746 (mixed)
   for WDW Banana
   Popsicle

1 WDW 1115 Banana Popsicle
2 DMC 310 black, dots
3 DMC 310 black
4 DMC 988 green
5 DMC 335 dark pink; inner line, DMC 815 dark red
6 DMC 553 purple; inner line, DMC 3326 pink
7 DMC 743 yellow; inner line, DMC 3853 bright orange
8 DMC 800 light blue; inner line, DMC 826 dark blue
9 DMC 817 dark red; inner line, DMC 3326 pink
10 DMC 922 light orange; inner line DMC 919 dark orange

Crossed Tulips

I love the look of a soft wool rug.

This is a great way to try different fibers—
you are not limited to using cotton floss.

This project looks great in a frame
or in an antique doll house.

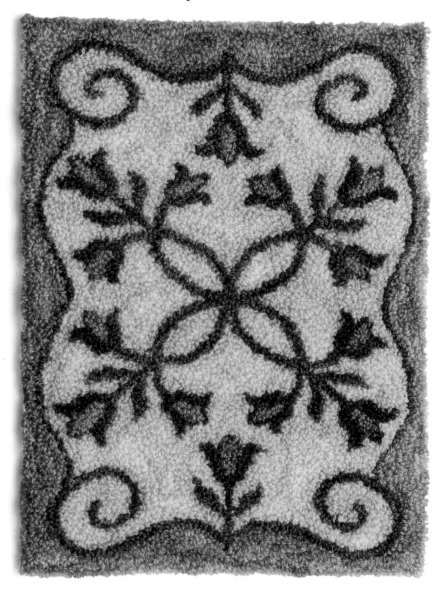

Not to scale. Actual size is 5¾" x 4⅛" (14.6 x 10.5 cm).

1. Trace the pattern to the weaver's cloth. Place the design so that the weft of the fabric is vertical and the warp is horizontal. (See diagram.)

2. Place the fabric in the hoop or frame with the design facing up. Make sure the fabric is pulled drum tight. You will be working from the back to the front.

3. Separate the nine-strand wool floss down to one strand. (One strand of Lorikeet wool is equivalent to three strands of cotton floss.)

4. Adjust the needle for a ⅜" (1 cm) gauge. Punch areas 1 to 5 in order. Refer to the numbered chart for the placement of each color.

5. Rake the loops (page 22) into place for a nice sharp image.

Materials

three-strand punchneedle

weaver's cloth

3½" (8.9 cm) curved-tip scissors

8" (20.3 cm) hoop

**Gloriana Threads
(9-strand Lorikeet wool):**

105A Taupe Light,

128B Cherry Tart Light,

120D Green Gables Medium Dark,

089W3 Twilight,

089W4 Twilight Dark

1	105A Taupe Light	4	089W4 Twilight Dark
2	128B Cherry Tart Light	5	089W3 Twilight
3	120D Green Gables Medium Dark		

Trio of Hearts

Treasured Heart

Treasured Heart was inspired by a keepsake,
heart-shaped necklace that was made out of
a broken antique plate and set in sterling silver.

Stained Glass Heart

One Christmas, my dad made gifts
for each of his girls.
When I look at this happy heart
with its bold colors,
I can't help but think of the
beautiful stained glass lamps
we each pulled out of our gift boxes.

Heart within My Heart

Heart within My Heart describes the joy
that punchneedle embroidery
has brought to me.

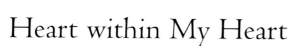

Not to scale. Actual size is 1½" x 3" (3.8 x 7.6 cm).

FOR ALL

1. Trace the pattern to the weaver's cloth. Place the design so that the weft of the fabric is horizontal and the warp is vertical. (See diagram.)

2. Place the fabric in the hoop or frame with the design facing up. Make sure the fabric is pulled drum tight. You will be working from the back to the front.

3. Separate the six-strand floss into two three-strand units.

FOR TREASURED HEART

4. Adjust the needle for a ⅜" (1 cm) gauge. Punch area 1. Refer to the numbered chart (page 64) for the placement of each color.

5. Adjust the needle for a ½" (2.5 cm) gauge. Punch areas 2 and 3 in order.

FOR STAINED GLASS HEART

4. Adjust the needle for a ⅜" (1 cm) gauge. Punch area 1. Refer to the numbered chart for the placement of each color.

5. Adjust the needle for a ½" (1.3 cm) gauge. Punch areas 2 to 6 in order.

FOR HEART WITHIN MY HEART

4. Adjust the needle for a ⅜" (1 cm) gauge. Punch area 1. Refer to the numbered chart for the placement of each color.

5. Adjust the needle for a ½" (1.3 cm) gauge. Punch areas 2 to 4 in order.

FOR ALL

6. Rake the loops (page 22) into place for a nice sharp image.

Materials for all
three-strand punchneedle
weaver's cloth (natural)
3½" (8.9 cm)
curved-tip scissors
6" (15.2 cm) hoop

Treasured Heart:
DMC Floss:
815 red and 3825 gold

Weeks Dye Works Floss:
3900 Kohl black/gray (2)

Stained Glass Heart:
DMC Floss:
163 green, 311 blue, 815 red, 3023 taupe, and 3825 gold

Weeks Dye Works Floss:
3900 Kohl black/gray (2)

Heart within My Heart:
DMC Floss:
815 red and 3825 gold

Weeks Dye Works Floss:
3900 Kohl black/gray (2)

Substitution:
DMC 310 for WDW Kohl

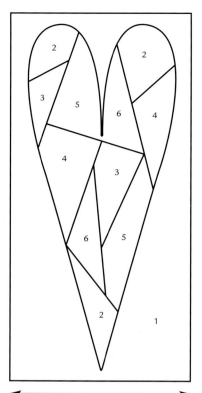

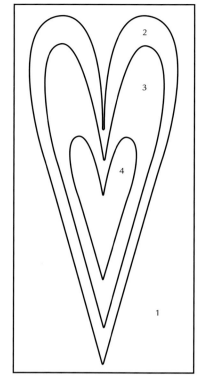

Treasured Heart

1 WDW 3900 Kohl black/gray
2 DMC 815 red
3 DMC 3825 gold

Stained Glass Heart

1 Weeks Dye Works
  3900 Kohl black/gray
2 DMC 815 red
3 DMC 311 blue
4 DMC 163 green
5 DMC 3825 gold
6 DMC 3023 taupe

Heart within My Heart

1 WDW 3900 Kohl black/gray
2 DMC 815 red
3 DMC 3825 gold
4 DMC 815 red

FINISHING & FRAMING

EYEGLASS BAG

Punchneedle designs can be worked directly onto fabric that you then make into a useful or decorative item. As an example, this eyeglass bag features the Blooming Heart design from page 42. The bag is fully lined, which protects the back of the design. Because weaver's cloth comes in an assortment of colors as well as white, you can use it as a background for your project. If you choose to punch your design on a different fabric, such as linen or cotton, stabilize it first with fusible interfacing.

Materials

template plastic or heavy paper

weaver's cloth (linen) or other fabric

Form Flex All Purpose fusible interfacing, optional

Blooming Heart pattern, page 89

threads and supplies as listed on page 43

scissors

sewing machine

hand-sewing needle and thread

1 yd. (0.92 m) cording

liquid fray preventer

1. Enlarge the bag template below or draw a rectangle 2" x 7¾" (12.7 x 19.7 cm) and round the two corners as shown. Trace it onto template plastic or heavy paper. Trace the outline onto the weaver's cloth or fused interfacing; then flip the template, line up the fold line, and trace the other side. Repeat to mark a piece for the bag back.

2. Trace the Blooming Heart pattern onto the wrong side of the bag front, centering the design with the bottom at least 1½" (3.8 cm) from the bottom of the bag. Do not cut out the bag front until it is punched. You need extra fabric to put the design in the hoop. Punch the design, following the directions on page 43.

3. Remove the design from the hoop, and block it (page 22).

4. Cut out the front and back of the bag. Fold each piece in half, wrong sides together.

5. Place the front and the back right sides together, and pin around the cut edges. Sew the two pieces together with a ¼" (6 mm) seam allowance, backstitching at the folds. Do not sew along the folds. Turn the bag right side out.

6. Determine how long you want the cording. Apply liquid fray preventer to the cording where you intend to cut it, and allow it to dry. Then cut the cording.

7. Tuck the cord ends into the bag at the sides. Stitch the cording to the seam allowances. Stitch the top folds of the bag around the cording at each side.

TIP

If using fabric other than weaver's cloth, trace the template and pattern onto fusible interfacing. Then fuse interfacing to the wrong side of the fabric in an area larger than the hoop.

FOLD

BAG TEMPLATE (enlarge 200%)

FABRIC FRAMES

Make soft, flexible fabric frames for your designs using felted wool or other coordinating fabric. Add a cord or narrow ribbon hanger, and use the framed design as a Christmas ornament or doorknob hanger. Frame two finished pieces back to back, and hang them from a ceiling fan. Without the hanger, your framed design can be stitched to a basket or glued to the top of a keepsake box. Applying glue only to the backing fabric protects your heirloom.

Materials

felted wool or other fabric that coordinates with your design

template plastic

fusible stabilizer

liquid fray preventer

embroidery floss

size 22 tapestry needle

thimble

Pigma pen

scissors

FIGURE 1

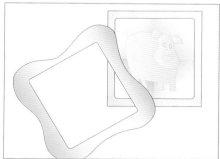

FIGURE 2

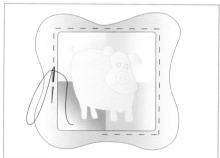

FIGURE 3

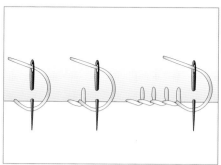

FIGURE 4

1. Punch the design, following the project directions. Remove the design from the hoop, and block it (page 22).

2. Measure the design, and draw a rectangle the same size on paper. Then draw the desired shape for your frame around the rectangle. Trace the shape on template plastic, and cut it out.

3. Using the template, trace two shapes on the fusible stabilizer, and cut them out.

4. Draw an opening the size of the design in the center of one of the pieces of stabilizer. This will be the frame front.

5. Using an iron, fuse the stabilizer pieces to the wrong side of the frame fabric. Allow it to cool.

6. Cut out the frame front and back ⅛" (3 mm) larger than the stabilizer. Set the back aside for now.

7. Cut out the center of the frame front. If you are using wool, cut the opening slightly smaller than the drawn line. (Remember, you can always go back and make the opening a little bigger, but you can't make it smaller if you cut it too big.) The wool will stretch slightly and give it a tight fit. Check to see if it fits tightly around the design. [FIGURE 1]

8. Lightly trace around the frame on the weaver's cloth. Remove the frame, and cut the weavers cloth about ½" (1.3 cm) beyond the design, making sure the edges are inside the traced frame. [FIGURE 2]

9. Sign and date your project along the back edge of the weaver's cloth.

10. Place the wool frame over the punched design. Make sure no loops are caught under the edges. Thread a tapestry needle with six strands of floss. Sew the frame to the weaver's cloth border, using a large running stitch about ¼" (6 mm) from the edge of the opening. Or stitch a decorative stitch with your sewing machine. Be careful not to catch the loops as you sew. [FIGURE 3]

11. Stitch a cording or ribbon hanger to the back of the frame. If you are using cording, apply liquid fray preventer to the ends before cutting it to the correct length.

12. Place the front and back frame pieces wrong sides together. Pin in place. Trim around the outside edges, if necessary, so that the pieces match perfectly.

13. Stitch the front to the back with a blanket stitch around the outer edge of the frame. [FIGURE 4]

TIP

I don't recommend using glue with your projects but if you do, use only acid-free, lignin-free glue. Check the ingredients on the glue bottle.

MOUNTING IN A PRESET OPENING

Needle art companies produce lots of very creative and useful products with openings designed to show off your punchneedle designs. There are decorative boxes, fashion pin and pendant backs, clocks, mirrors, dowry boxes, and needle cases to name a few. Be sure to choose a design that will fit the opening. The size required should be indicated on the package, or you can measure the opening from the front. Before you pop it in place, you need to mount your design on mat board.

Materials
ruler
mat board
    (without adhesive)
craft knife
pearl cotton, size 8
size 22 tapestry needle
Pigma pen
Pellon fleece, optional

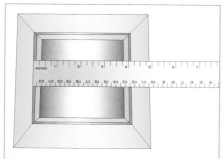

FIGURE 1

FIGURE 2

FIGURE 3

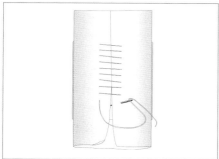

FIGURE 4

1. If the item you buy does not include a mat board, measure the opening. For box lids, measure from the back. The opening usually has a lip that is at least ½" (1.3 cm) larger than the opening from the front of the lid. For items without a lip, simply measure the opening. [FIGURE 1]

2. Cut a piece of mat board slightly smaller than the measured opening, using a craft knife. This will allow you to wrap the fabric over the sides to the back.

3. Punch the design, following the project directions. Remove the design from the hoop, and block it (page 22.)

4. For mounting in a box lid, the finished design should be ½" (1.3 cm) smaller than the mat board. This allows for a ¼" (6 mm) margin around the design where it fits under the lip of the opening. For openings without a lip, the design should be the same size as the mat board. Center the design and place it into the opening to make sure the design is large enough for the opening. [FIGURE 2]

5. Cut a piece of fleece the same size as the design to layer between the design and mat board if you want to create a slightly padded appearance. [FIGURE 3]

6. Trim the weaver's cloth so that, when folded to the back of the mat board, the edges do not overlap.

7. Center the design on the board (with optional fleece between them), and wrap the excess fabric at the sides to the back. Thread a tapestry needle with pearl cotton, and knot the end. Beginning near the top, take large stitches from left to right, lacing the sides together tightly. Check from the front to make sure the design is still centered and adjust, if necessary. [FIGURE 4]

8. Wrap the excess fabric at the top and bottom to the back, and lace the edges together as in step 7.

9. Sign and date your project on the back.

10. Insert the mounted design into the opening. Boxes may have a backing board to secure in place. If inserting into a pin or pendant back, glue the design in place with a few dots of acid-free, lignin-free glue.

TIP
If the design is too small and you can see weaver's cloth, place the design back into the hoop and punch another row around the outside.

MOUNTING ON FOAM CORE BOARD

This technique can be used to mount a design that has been punched on colored weaver's cloth into a decorative frame, with or without additional matting. The border of exposed weaver's cloth accents your design. You can also use this method to cover foam core board with a background fabric for mounting in a frame. Then you can appliqué (page 80) your design to the background or mount it using archival framing methods (page 78).

Materials

silk pins
ruler
acid-free foam core board,
    ¼" (6 mm) thick
craft knife
Pigma pen
Pellon fleece, optional
thimble, optional

FIGURE 1

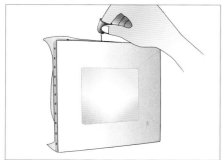

FIGURE 2

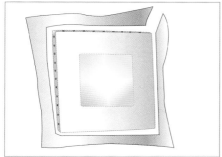

FIGURE 3

1. Punch the design on colored weaver's cloth, following the project directions. Remove the design from the hoop, and block it (page 22).

2. Measure the opening of the back of the frame. The opening has a lip that is at least ½" (1.3 cm) larger than the opening from the front of the frame.

3. Cut acid-free foam core board slightly smaller than the measured opening, using a craft knife. This allows room for the fabric to wrap over the sides and for pin heads.

4. Cut a piece of fleece the same size as the mounting board if you want the design to have a slightly padded appearance.

5. Center the design on the board (with optional fleece between them). Insert pins through the fabric and into the foam core at the four corners and at the center of each side. This will keep the design from moving. Measure to make sure the design is still centered. [FIGURE 1]

6. Stand the board on one edge. Pull the fabric over the opposite edge, and pin it in place, pinning into the edge of the foam core. Work from the center out to each end, spacing the pins ⅜" to ½" (1 to 1.3 cm) apart. Use a thimble to protect your finger. [FIGURE 2]

7. Repeat step 6 on the remaining three sides, checking occasionally to make sure the design is still centered.

8. Place the design in the frame opening. Adjust if necessary.

9. Trim away excess fabric even with the back of the foam core board. [FIGURE 3]

10. Insert precut matting into the frame, if desired. Then insert the mounted design into the frame opening.

11. Sign and date your project on the back.

FINISH WITH CORDING

You can mount any design with a padded front and padded, fabric-covered back. To make it suitable for hanging, invisibly stitch twisted cording around the edge with a loop at the top and perhaps a knot and tassel at the bottom. You can purchase narrow cording or make your own using a special tool and extra floss that matches your project. Your work of art becomes a cherished ornament or mini wall hanging.

Materials
mat board
Pellon fleece
scissors
size 22 tapestry needle
pearl cotton size #8
fabric to coordinate with the design
size 7 embroidery needle
invisible finishing thread or
    one strand of matching thread
cording or floss to make cording
Spinster, optional

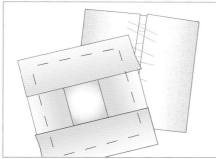

FIGURE 1

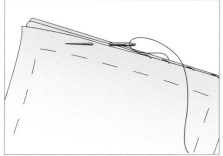

FIGURE 2

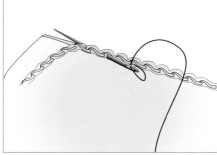

FIGURE 3

TIP

To finish a design with
a padded back but without
cording, stitch a loop of cording
or ribbon inside before placing
the front and back together.
When you stitch the backing
in place, be sure to stitch
as close to the design
as possible.

1. Punch the design, following the project directions. Make sure the last two rows of your punched design are close together. Remove the design from the hoop, and block it (page 22).

2. Measure the exact dimensions of the back of the design. Cut a piece of mat board and two pieces of fleece to this size.

3. Place one piece on the back of the design. Place the mat board on top. Make sure both pieces line up exactly to the edge of the design.

4. Trim the weaver's cloth 2" to 3" (5.1 to 7.6 cm) from the edge of the design. Thread the tapestry needle with pearl cotton, and lace the edges together at the back, as in steps 7 and 8 on page 71.

5. Sign and date your project on the back.

6. Cut a piece of coordinating fabric for the backing 3" (7.6 cm) larger than the measured design. Center the second piece of fleece on the wrong side of the fabric. Fold the fabric edges over the fleece so the fabric is slightly larger. Baste them in place. [FIGURE 1]

7. Place the backing over the back of the design with the folded edge up against the last row of loops, covering most of the weaver's cloth. Slipstitch the backing in place, using an embroidery needle and a single strand of thread. (The cording will hide any weaver's cloth that is still showing.) Remove the basting. [FIGURE 2]

8. Make your own cording or use purchased cording. You'll need enough to go around the design with extra length for tying a loop and tassel.

9. Fold the cording in half. Tie a knot, forming a loop of the desired size for hanging.

TIP

I like to make my own
cording using a great little
gadget called a Spinster. Use
floss from your design for a
perfect match, and follow
the directions that come
with the Spinster.

10. Center the knot at the top of your design. Using the invisible finishing thread and the embroidery needle, begin stitching the cording to the edge of the design on one side of the top knot. Run the needle between the twists in the cord; then take a tiny stitch in the edge of the design, advancing the needle to the next location where it can again be inserted between the twists in the cord. This will hide the stitch and secure the cording to the edge of the design. Continue around the design, stopping at the bottom center. [FIGURE 3]

11. Begin again at the knot, and stitch the cording to the opposite side of the design. Tie the ends together in a knot snug to the bottom of the design. Secure in place with small stitches inside the knot.

12. Cut the cording ends leaving tails. Allow the tails to unwind, forming a tassel. Trim the tassel to the desired length.

WHIPSTITCHED EDGE

Whipstitching finishes the edge of your design with a neat, distinct ridge. Using floss in the same colors as the border of the design blends the whipstitched edge into the design. For a contrasting border, combine strands of different colors or choose a color from the interior of the design.

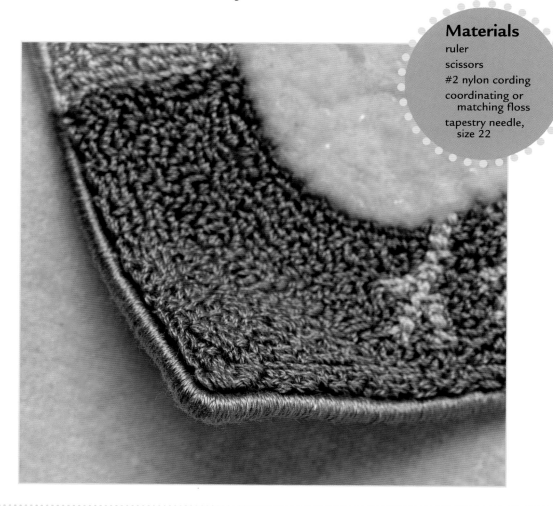

Materials

ruler

scissors

#2 nylon cording

coordinating or matching floss

tapestry needle, size 22

TIP

If you are using overdyed floss, flip two of the four strands in the opposite direction. This blends the color tones and prevents distinct color changes as you whipstitch.

1. Punch the design, following the project directions. Remove the design from the hoop, and block it (page 22).

2. Trim the weaver's cloth 2" (5.1 cm) from the edge of the design.

3. Cut the floss into 12" (30.5 cm) lengths. (It will get tangled too easily if it is much longer.) Separate the floss one strand at a time. Thread the tapestry needle with four strands of floss.

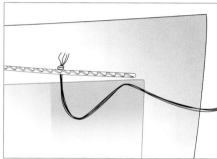

FIGURE 1 (back)

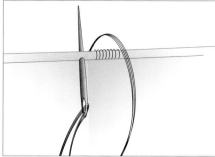

FIGURE 2 (front)

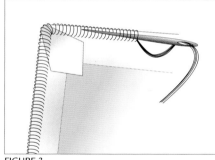

FIGURE 3

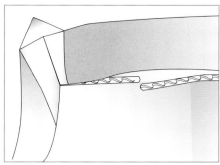

FIGURE 4

4. Tie the floss strands together with a small knot at one end. Stitch the floss through the nylon cording about 2" (5.1 cm) from the end. From the reverse side, insert the needle near the edge of the design where you want to start whipstitching, and pull the floss through to the front. This will keep the cording from moving as you stitch around the design. Always start along a straight side, never at a corner. [FIGURE 1]

5. Hold the cording along the edge of the design on the reverse side. Roll the weaver's cloth snugly over the cording, and hold it in place on the back. Insert the needle from front to back close to the edge, forming a short running stitch (just to get the needle to the back).

6. Bring the needle to the front, and insert it again at the edge of the design at your starting point; bring it out on the back. The floss wraps over the covered cording, forming a whipstitch. Always insert the needle from the front. (If you go from back to front, you risk coming up into the loops and snagging the threads.)

7. Continue whipstitching over the covered cording, placing your stitches right next to each other. If you are right-handed, whipstitch around the design counterclockwise. If you are left-handed, whipstitch around the design clockwise. The strands of floss should lie flat next to each other and cover the edge evenly. [FIGURE 2]

8. Stop stitching about ½" (1.3 cm) from each corner. Crease the cording at the point where it will turn the corner, and hold it for 30 seconds. When you let go, the cording will naturally bend around the corner. Fold small tucks in the weaver's cloth so it wraps over the cording in a smooth, snug curve around the corner. Continue whipstitching.

9. When you need to change colors or begin a new length of floss, run the needle under the stitches for about ½" (1.3 cm) on the reverse side. Cut the floss, and remove the needle. Rethread the needle. Take a tiny stitch on the back or run the needle under the previous stitches to secure the end. Then begin again as in step 6. [FIGURE 3]

10. As you approach the beginning, cut the end of the cording so it just meets the beginning end. Tuck the ends back under the weaver's cloth, and finish whipstitching. End the floss as in step 9. [FIGURE 4]

11. On the back of the design, trim away excess weaver's cloth from the four corners to allow the design to lie flat. Your design is now ready to be mounted.

> **TIP**
> If the floss becomes twisted, the stitches will be bumpy. Let the needle hang to untwist the floss after every fourth stitch.

ARCHIVAL FRAMING

You have just created an heirloom that will be admired for generations to come. You'll want to finish it to last. Chemicals in glue can cause the design to become discolored or even break down the fiber in your design. With archival framing, the design is attached to a mounting board with stitches. You can simply snip threads to remove it if you change your mind about the background or want to use the design in another way.

Materials

#2 nylon cording
acid-free foam core board
background fabric/wool
coordinating or matching floss
black felt
size 22 tapestry needle
thimble
ruler
craft knife
silk pins
scissors

1. Punch the design, following the project directions. Remove the design from the hoop, and block it (page 22).

2. Whipstitch the outer edge of the design (page 76), if desired. Otherwise, trim the weaver's cloth to within ½" (1.3 cm) of the design.

3. Cover acid-free foam core board with background fabric, following the directions on page 72.

4. Center the finished design on the covered foam core board. If you have not whipstitched the edge, fold under the margin of weaver's cloth. Secure the design temporarily with silk pins in each corner.

5. Cut eight small squares of black felt. Thread a tapestry needle with two strands of floss. The floss doesn't need to match to the design because your stitches will be hidden down in the pile.

6. Place a felt square on the back of the foam core board, lining it up with one corner of the design. Stitch into the felt through the foam core board and through the inside corner of the design. Pull the thread all the way through. Insert the needle tip close to where the thread comes out and stitch back through the design, mounting board, and felt. Angle your needle so it exits the felt at a spot about ½" (1.3 m) from where it went in. [FIGURE 1]

7. Continue to stitch the design using a square of felt in each corner and at the center of each side. [FIGURE 2]

8. If you did not whipstitch the edge of your design, you can cover the exposed edge with narrow cording or other trim, invisibly hand-stitching it in place.

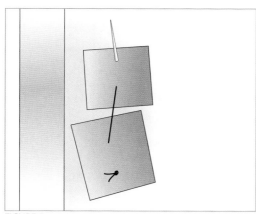

FIGURE 1

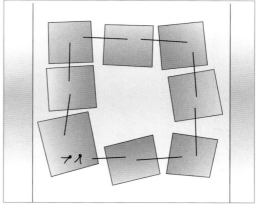

FIGURE 2

APPLIQUÉ FINISHING

A finished design can be appliquéd to another fabric or fabric item, such as a ready-made pillow, a tote bag, or a pocket.

Materials

size 20 embroidery needle

thimble

coordinating fabric or fabric item

floss (for securing design with whipstitched edge)

invisible finishing thread (for securing design with plain edge)

scissors

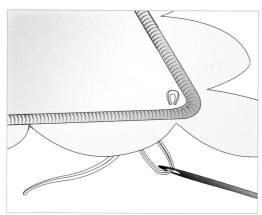

FIGURE 1

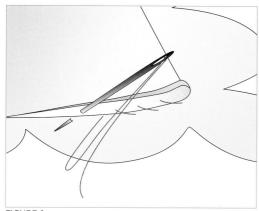

FIGURE 2

1. Punch the design, following the project directions. Remove the design from the hoop, and block it (page 22). Follow the instructions for a whipstitched edge, or just trim the weaver's cloth and turn it back to expose only the design.

2. Center the design on the fabric, and pin it in place.

3. If your design has a whipstitched edge, stitch the design to the fabric background with small stitches between the whipstitching and the design edge. Use two strands of floss threaded on the embroidery needle. The floss doesn't need to match to the design because the stitches will be hidden in the pile. [FIGURE 1]

If the edge is not whipstitched, use invisible thread to blindstitch the design to the fabric. [FIGURE 2]

RESOURCES

Check out your local needlework shop for all your punchneedle supplies. Visit my website at www.russianpunchneedle.com. For a shop near you, click on "Find a Shop."

Punchneedle Patterns Plus
A source for all your punchneedle patterns, supplies, and accessories.
www.punchneedlepatternsplus.com

METAL PUNCHNEEDLES
Bernadine's Punch Needles
Bernadine's Needle Art
PO Box 287
Arthur, Il 61911

CTR Punch Embroidery Needles
CTR Inc.
1334 Indian Creek Valley Road
PO Box 154
Melcroft, PA 15462

Igolochkoy
Birdhouse Enterprises
4438 G Street
Sacramento, CA 95819

PLASTIC PUNCHNEEDLES
Cameo Ultra Punch
Distributed in the United States by Brohman's Inc.
333-335 Pam Drive
Derrien Springs, MI 49103

Clover Embroidery Stitching Tool
Clover Needlecraft Inc.
13438 Alondra Blvd.
Cerritos, CA 90703

SUPPLIES
Bizzi Creations, Inc.
1861 Brown Blvd
Suite 217-625
Arlington, TX 76006
bizzicreations@att.net
www.bizzicreations.com
4" x 4" (10.2 x 10.2 cm) red box, page 70

Hog River Frames
hogonalog@aol.com
#49 white polka dots on pastel green,
5" x 5" (12.7 x 12.7 cm), page 78

Susan Ebright
Needle Art and Interior Design
Trail Creek Farm
1355 15th Road
Lyons, KS 67554
620-257-2577
susan@trailcreekfarm.com
www.trailcreekfarm.com
purple ready-made bag, page 80

Twisted Threads
9 DePaul Hills Court
Bridgeton, MO 63044
314-739-2022
www.twistedthreads.com
tin frames, page 70

Olde Colonial Designs
P.O. Box 704
Marshfield, MA 02050
781-834-8836
stitches@adelphia.net
www.oldecolonialdesigns.com
items with openings for mounting designs

Pellon Products (fleece and craft fuse)
4720A Stone Drive
Tucker, GA 30084
www.ShopPellon.com
Check out your local fabric store.

HTCW , Inc.
Form-Flex All Purpose (fabric stabilizer)
Creative Interfacing Products
103 Eisenhower Pkwy.
Roseland, NJ 07068

Springs Global US, Inc (weaver's cloth)
"Weaver's" Natural
Rock Hill, SC 29730
Check out your local fabric and craft stores.

K's Creations
www.kscreations.com
800-727-3769
stretcher frame for punchneedls

Susan Bates Hoop-La
Available at many needlework and craft stores
lip edge hoops

Morgan Hoops & Stands Inc.
info@nosliphoops.com
314-540-1717
Available at many needlework and craft stores
tongue and groove hoops

Gingher Scissors
www.gingher.com
gingherinfor@gingher.com
800-446-4437
G-446, 3½" (8.9 cm) curved-tip scissors

RECOMMENDED READING
Jim Rearden (photographs by Charles O'Rear), "A Bit of Old Russia Takes Root in Alaska,"
National Geographic 142, no. 3 (1972).

RECOMMENDED VIDEO
Punchneedle Embroidery by Charlotte Dudney
This video presentation on DVD contains approximately one hour of detailed instruction.
I cover the Sunflower project (included) from start to finish, as well as finishing techniques
and problems and solutions. The DVD comes with the Sunflower pattern printed on weaver's
cloth, as well as three original designs to print and trace from your computer. Jump from
chapter to chapter for a quick reference.

ABOUT THE AUTHOR

Charlotte Dudney is a nationally recognized punchneedle teacher who also designs under the business name
Designs from the Pep'r Pot. She learned about punchneedle at a rug hooking camp years ago. Charlotte began
designing patterns with printed fabric included. Her "no tracing required" patterns have been well received,
and she now has over 80 original designs on the market. You can see her designs on her Web site:
www.russianpunchneedle.com.

Charlotte lives in Arlington, Texas with her husband, Fred. She travels extensively, teaching and promoting
the art form. She has taught thousands of people in over a dozen states. Hundreds of shop owners have learned
about punchneedle, and many are now holding classes themselves. She has been a featured teacher at International
Needleart Retailers Guild and the National NeedleArts Association Markets in 2004, 2005, 2006, and 2007.
Charlotte holds "virtual classes" daily since the release of her popular instructional DVD, *Punchneedle Embroidery,*
in 2004. She loves to teach in Austin, Texas, where her travel always includes a wonderful visit with her daughter.

PATTERNS

Westie On Alert

Laura *Note:* To use this silhouette, trace it before stretching the fabric in the hoop.

Peep, Peep

Baa, Baa, Black Sheep

This Little Piggy

Heart within my Heart

Treasured Love

Stained Glass Heart

Guardian Angel

Blooming Heart

Bunny

Bless Our Home

Duncan

Spring

Summer

Fall

Winter

This Is Not a Partridge

Crossed Tulips

Bouquet of Flowers